My Vacuum Sucks

Humorous Essays Written While Going
from Office Zombie, to Stay-at-Home
Dad, to Educator

By Brett Chrest

September 2021

Thesan Press

ISBN (eBook):   978-1-7377610-0-6

ISBN (Paperback): 978-1-7377610-1-3

ISBN (Hard cover): 978-1-7377610-2-0

Thesan Press

thesanpress@gmail.com

To my wife and children, who started me on this road, inspired and encouraged my creativity, and saw me across the finish line.

Thank you.

Table of Contents

"Stories have to be told or they die, and when they die, we can't remember who we are or why we are here." - Sue Monk Kidd

Introduction

I have had people say to me – somewhat skeptically at times - "You have a story for everything!" It is true. I tell a lot of stories. But it is not because I have a weird and/or interesting life. The key to having stories is to be observant enough to know when you are in one. Stories are indiscriminate, they will visit themselves upon anyone – from cradle to grave – who cares enough to experience them.

We are born with stories to tell from the womb, although we do not yet know how to perceive them or how to communicate them. That comes over time as we learn to interact with others while learning who we are from the stories of those who came before us.

Stories still visited my grandmother, even at the end when she was too weak to talk most of the time. She was still able to receive visits from her great-grandchildren and hear the oldest go on and on about what they had been up to recently. If there is good in this world, she was able to tell at least one story about them and, like any expert storyteller, included a slight embellishment or two.

Embellishment is something that comes with age, a slight adjustment upwards in length of travel, hurdles conquered, and the like. Embellishment, however, is never lying. Lying makes the teller more than who/what they are. Embellishment adds a touch of the surreal to the story. It is a little bit of myth. "I drove to McDonald's." vs. "Why, I was so hungry that I drove 50 miles – running every stop sign I found – to get to that McDonald's." In this way, the teller almost becomes immortal, kept alive by their stories as they themselves become part of someone else's.

I wrote all these stories down during a period of transition. I was leaving a soul-eating career for one that had always been a passion of mind. As a happy by-product, I had plenty of time to reflect and to write. This is a roster of – hopefully – humorous stories/essays that came to me as I reflected on that unique season of life. I have written other more serious writings as well, but they are for another book. Those will not appear here.

The funny and the serious sides all share something in common (aside from me being the author): they are all about being content while existing in the present, and not always as being obsessed with where your next step will land.

All of these are true; even the story about writing a "fake" story.

They reflect a newfound appreciation for observation and the reception of the stories which fly around all of us. It is a window into contentment with who I am, what I am, and where I am.

If this collection fails to illustrate the beautiful absurdity of human life, at least by the end of it all, you will have a few good poop jokes to whip out at the next wedding reception you have to attend.

-n.b.c. September 2021

Grilling

"When I figured out how to work my grill, it was quite a moment. I discovered that summer is a completely different experience when you know how to grill."
- Taylor Swift

Rorik of Dorestad looked out over an angry sea. As the waves crashed into the rocky shore, the Viking priests made their final preparations and lifted Eric Bloodaxe's body onto the pyre. With a wave of Rorik's hand, the high priest lit the fire. Eric was a good warrior – he had truly earned the surname of Bloodaxe. Even in the time of the Vikings, the burning of dead flesh over an open fire – grilling – was viewed as a sacred rite. Nobody ate anything though. The smell was awful.

Today, we keep that ancient tradition alive. Only now we do not cook our war buddies when they die. Instead, we use lots of lighter fluid and little black briquettes to heat the interior temperature of a dead chicken, cow, etc. to a level that is safe for human consumption. If people – especially priests – are around to share with, so much the better. The backyard BBQ is as quintessentially suburban as distracted driving. The ability to host a good 'que is the most important social skill a suburbanite can have. It all starts with the most basic BBQ fare: the burger.

After years of refining the task, I have become quite good at grilling burgers. Even people who do not have a personal stake in saying pleasant things about my cooking (like my kids) compliment them. Some of these steps might seem odd, but as Aristotle once said (probably) "don't knock it 'til you try it." Spending so much time to produce this list was a labor of love. Standing in front of searing meat gets me closer to my true self.

Step One: Burger King

Let us be honest: any of the following steps can go sideways in a hurry. The most common cause of a disrupted plan are what I call the Three Ws: weather, wildlife and winos.

"Hey gang, burgers are going to be a little delayed – Mike got third degree burns after face planting into the grill, but there's still plenty of chips and dip!"

So, if you are counting on getting grilled beef in front of an audience, it is best to proactively have a back-up plan. As far as I can tell, scraping the patty off a Burger King burger, and onto your own bun has the greatest chance for success in fooling your guests. But let's stay optimistic and hope we do not get to that point.

Step Two: The Grill

This is important! Even if you are sure you will need Burger King to fool your guests into thinking that you grilled a burger, you need to have a grill on your property for them to see. A grilled burger without any evidence of a grill will immediately be seen as fraudulent.

So, get a grill. Even if you only ever use it to fake-grill, it looks kind of pretty. While shopping for a grill (which you actually plan to use as nature intended) the high-end propane models with multiple heating platforms seem pretty swell. No, a side burner does nothing to help your burger grilling skill and it rarely works more than three times (if you are lucky). Even if properly working, it merely warms up baked beans, or, if it is a chilly evening, your hands.

All you need is a structure that can hold charcoal, handle elevated temperatures, and has a rack to hold the meat. Dials and gauges are fool's gold. Just like the superfluous side burner, they'll break within the first month.

Step Three: Prepping the Meat

We can quibble over the best fat/meat ratio for ground beef, or even whether or not veggie burgers are cool (they are). We cannot, however, quibble over the fact that whatever you are using for your burger needs to be withdrawn from its refrigerated storage at least an hour before hitting the grill rack. Tossing a cold patty

11

on a hot grill is just setting yourself up for some tragically uneven cooking.

Once that meat warms up a bit, it is ready for pre-seasoning. When you have a chunk of ground beef, it is key to knead the seasoning into the meat before you form the patties. This means that your seasoning — I use Old Bay since I am from Maryland — can get to all parts of the beef when you start to break it up, and massage it into burger form. You can even use herbs. Oregano is fun. Parsley works.

Thyme? No way! And if you decide to spice a patty or two up with cayenne pepper, make sure to remember which patty is which. It is not cool to inadvertently surprise a guest.

Be patient and do not form the patties quite yet — let that seasoning settle for a bit.

Step Four: Starting the Grill

This step seems straightforward: dunk some charcoal into a grill, toss on 7.2 gallons of lighter fluid, light a match, and see if the International Space Station can see your cauldron of flame. But there is some (albeit not much) nuance here. For one, you might have noticed that forming the patties has not happened yet. This is because you are going to need plenty of time to burn off all that lighter fluid. Also, it is important to manage your charcoal distribution.

The coals ought not be equally dispersed throughout the base of the grill. Instead, keep them to one side. This will help when the meat hits the rack in terms of meat placement and temperature control. I am a strong proponent of the "Meat Shuffle" approach and not the "Place, Cover, and Forget" method.

Step Five: Patty Time

Now that your beef has been hanging out with your seasoning for a bit, while you got your grill all hot and bothered, you can make those patties. I shoot for 5″ across and about 3/4 of an inch thick. Of course, this is after a robust massaging session for each patty to make sure that it is properly formed, and that the seasoning is equally dispersed throughout.

If you do not have time to massage your meat, I can't really help you. You must seize control of time management.

I typically only form and grill 4–5 patties at a time since, as mentioned, I only have coals over half of the grill.

Step Six: Meat Meets Fire

So, we have the patties — seasoned and formed, and we have a grill hot enough to handle the task of making a perfect burger. Now, it is time that the two meet.

For the next several minutes of your life, your burgers will need your love and attention. Since I use the half-grill approach (only putting coals on one side of the grill and actually placing the meat on the other side), my grilling takes longer. But, as I move the patties over various parts of the rack without coals underneath, I can maintain juiciness while also keeping a slow cook. This, of course, requires multiple flips.

I like to go five to seven minutes a side, with at least three flips and additional grilling as I see fit. As mentioned, this takes more time, but it is worth it in the end.

One-flippers have no idea what they are doing. Or they just do not care.

When my burgers are done and off the grill, they have a smoke ring that screams flavor. (It is flavorful — I do not mean that the meat literally yells "FLAVOR!")

Step Seven: Boat that Bass, You Did It

While grilling — and I know that this is a lot to ask — you must keep the goal in focus. Sadly, you need to juggle multiple tasks to ensure proper timing and presentation. It is essential to monitor the meat while concurrently preparing the presentation. The worst burgers in the world are those that have cold, flaccid cheese draped over their shoulders. Get that dairy product queued up ahead of time, so that the heat of the meat can comfortably meld with the cheese. While the cheese melts, it is a suitable time to toast up some rolls. You can even put out the plate of non-animal fixings and/or condiments.

There you go: you have a plate full of nicely done burgers. You used an appropriate grill to cook a rational amount of meat. You tossed that meat onto prepared rolls, probably along with a slice of cheese. Now, all that is left is to let your guests go nuts and drown in juiciness. Sure, some people are savages and add things like carrots to their burger. Let it ride. God will judge them in the afterlife.

And if you have any leftover lettuce or tomato? Just chuck it into the yard. The rabbits will eat it (and then the foxes will eat the rabbits).

The Weather

I mentioned the "Three W's" that are the most common hurdles to a smooth BBQ. Two of these – wildlife and winos – are issues that you really can't do much with. Seriously, are you going to chase away a family of bear that surround your grill to watch their cubs play in your hot tub? And if Uncle Frank is too loaded to stay upright when he arrives, can you really salvage his afternoon in time? But weather...with preparedness and a good plan, you can handle freak weather events.

On one occasion, my wife obtained two hefty filets from a shockingly willing cow (or the grocery store — I forget which). That night, I decided to run them over the old' Weber. It had been a while since I did some nice steaks so I dusted off my standard play book and set about getting ready.

Any good plan requires precise timing, and accounts for any contingency. Pre-positioned first aid, for example, is essential in case a neighbor's yappy dog distracts you when you are igniting the grill. This is when you are most vulnerable.

Like any true American, even with steaks, I use an obnoxious amount of lighter fluid. If some dog started yapping at a jogger checking his/her progress on their wrist-worn fitness tracker, I could incinerate my arm. The good news is that, with so much fluid, I must give it ample time to burn off. Typically, we are looking at anywhere between 30 minutes and a month. This gives me plenty of time to tend to any third-degree burns.

The menu called for the steak (obviously), grill-baked potatoes, and grill-baked carrots. The potato factor meant that I'd have to tack on another hour to the process — those things resist heat like a champion. I can understand their moxie — they are adapted to grow in the soil. Soil is a solid that is considerably denser than air. Watermelons grow in the air. If one were to grill a watermelon — I cannot imagine why they would — it would succumb in less than three minutes.

I did not really care about the carrots. I don't like them. But my kids and wife do, so I took one for the team and tossed them into some foil with oil and seasoning.

After borrowing my wife's TI-83 graphing calculator (with a slide rule as backup), I was able to plot out a schedule for success. I am not sure what "cos" means, but pressing that button seemed to be helpful. (I briefly considered using "tan" — I do not want skin cancer and was unclear on how UV-ish its tan function was.) A few graphs later, complete with intersecting lines and a thorough analysis on the alternate exterior angles, I was ready to get going.

Weather in Maryland is notoriously fickle. To combat this, we have more meteorologists, per capita, than Tornado Alley. Everyone has their local favorite, and all the favorites helpfully post their own series of maps that purportedly show when harsh weather is set to strike the region. I thought that my (lengthy) plan fit into the window that my favorite had laid out.

My plan had a critical error: it did not factor in my proclivity for napping. When I arose from my slumber, I was already behind schedule. I rapidly prepared the meat and the vegetables (or fruits? who knows anymore — last week I learned that a pomegranate is actually in the "dinosaur" food group). The boys chipped in, and helpfully applied enormous amounts of salt to everything, including the kitchen counter. There was enough salt on various surfaces in that kitchen than an invading army of garden slugs would be stopped in their slimy tracks.

The skies were clear when I started the grill and retreated to the house to let 15.3 gallons of accelerant burn away. It was cloudy by the time I put on those stubborn potatoes and the crappy carrots. I knew doom was possible, but it still seemed off in the distance. I began to think that I might be able to pull this off without getting drenched and/or struck by lightning.

Then, doom.

A heavy rain started to fall, quickly followed by bright lightning, and cracks of thunder that rattled the bowels of our cats. I went into a "Don't Get Killed" delay.

I was not to be denied. Heroically, I got those steaks onto the grill in a fairly timely fashion. The worst had passed, but there was still some rumbling in the distance. I think one of the keys is to know when to divest yourself of long, metal grilling instruments/potential lightning rods. I loved He-Man growing up, and the idea of transforming into a superhero by getting struck by lightning intrigues me. Still, until sufficient scientific studies prove that method is safe, I'll refrain. Hopefully, now that the world's billionaires have all gone to space, they can focus their efforts and money into studying the He-Man Effect.

Even when I was confident that a powerful burst of electricity would not strike me and cause my heart to explode, it was still raining at a fast rate. This, of course, led to my wife and I getting drenched (she helpfully held the lid to the grill while I flipped the meat). I am not a fan of nature's brand of showers. The water is cold, the drops are big and sting-y, and mud gets splattered onto my feet and ankles. It was, however, fun for my oldest son to take pictures of mom and dad tending the grill while cats, dogs, and large turtles were falling from the sky. That scalawag has turned into quite the prolific photographer/paparazzo.

Even throughout all Nature threw at me, I presented perfectly cooked potatoes, meaningless carrots, which I assume were done, and two medium-rare filets. The two major food groups – meats and superfluous non-meats – were well represented.

My wife and the kids loved it. They even ate the carrots. I was more than happy to magnanimously "take one for the team" and offer my portion of orange plant matter. I was happy with the output as well.

Mostly, I was able to engender sympathy from my brood for braving a storm that could have produced large tornadoes (I mean, it could have happened. Nothing is impossible, right?) to put food on the family table. I hope the neighbors saw me as well.

"Look at that man of a man, standing like a granite sentinel in a maelstrom to battle the scourges of over-cooked steak!"

Traditions

As previously discussed, humankind has been relying on some form of a grill to cook meat for thousands of years; this far exceeds even the longest human life expectancies. So, it makes sense that a chain has remained unbroken over time with grill experts passing down their knowledge to the younger generation. Ever since the inventor of grilled meat painted a how-to on the walls of a cave in Northern Spain – the genesis of the modern-day DIY YouTube videos on properly spatchcocking a chicken – we have all enjoyed the benefits of 165+ degree dead animal flesh. Since that time, grilling has been the blood that nourished human civilization, even if the occasional conflict did arise:

"Forsooth, Father. I cannot tell a lie. This turkey is dryer than my wig." – George Washington

"Tell *me* how to grill 80/20 USDA ground beef? You got some nerve, Lincoln." – John Wilkes Booth

"We will show the capitalists that Korean BBQ is the one true BBQ! Viva North Korea!" – Kim Il-sung

Now, it is my turn to step into the great tradition of passing along the secrets of barbequeology (I have a Master of Science degree from Southern Pork University. (Go Flying (pork) Butts!). My oldest son just turned ten and it is time for him to begin his training. He must learn the deftness required to work the tongs and spatula. Master the art of swearing at the one damn hot dog that gets nudged up against the side of the grill and will not return to the center of the grate like his more cooperative brethren. In time, he will be able to discern done-ness simply by looking over the meat and/or injecting it with a thermometer probe that was curiously "invented" after the UFO crash in Roswell, NM. Someone will have to carry on the tradition in our family, and since Death could come calling at any moment, I am happy that we can share this passage of knowledge.

One cannot simply write such matters down, in the hopes that the finer points will survive a posthumous text review. You have to be out there, with the heat on your face and the grit of the patio beneath your feet. Only then does the learner experience the wholeness of the experience.

For his first outing, my oldest will be running with two 3/4″ thick fillets. This is a strong look – while fillets have mountains of flavor, they have a small and manageable surface area. This helps with seasoning and makes the meat considerably easier to move around the chess board that is a grill rack. If nothing else, my son will know that meat should never stay on the same side or the same spot on the grate for too long. In my advanced state of grilling, when I get aggressive and try to grill multiple types/cuts at once, I typically hire a local air traffic controller from nearby BWI airport for assistance.

"OK, we are going to vector lamb chop alpha north 2″ and slide lamb chop beta south-southwest .5″. Back fill LC alpha with pork chop theta and then.... why the hell is there an Etch-a-Sketch in Sector C?! Abort!"

22

Prep will be easy. Simply take the meat out of the fridge, remove it from its packaging and allow it to warm to room temperature (God bless thermodynamics!). Next, slather on a generous glug or two of EVOO, and season lightly. Oldest has a pretty free hand in the seasoning mixture, though I retain veto authority. A quarter cup of cayenne pepper per fillet seems a bit much. Neophyte seasoning errors are the third leading cause of death among "Mom, Dad – look what I made for you!" meals right behind salmonella and the inclusion of sharp LEGO parts. Those Danes make wonderful baked goods…and coldly efficient intestine-shredding plastic shapes.

I will handle the pyrotechnics. Over the years, I have gotten quite good at rapidly lighting my Weber 22″ grill in all kinds of weather. In addition to cooking meat and, for some reason (my wife's suggestion) grilled eggplant, we will, also, as previously discussed, grill some veggies. This means we will need at least three heating zones, each with their own specifications. It is unkind to expect him to nail coal placement so early in his rookie season, especially since he still asks basic questions.

"Dad, why do we need just a thin layer of ash on the coals? Isn't more heat better?"

"Ready you are not, padawan."

Then, it will be time to chat a bit while we wait for the accelerant to burn off and the coals to heat properly. After hearing all about the pros and cons of his new bike and the huge snake he and his friend found the other day, we will toss that beef onto the grill, and immediately spend 5+ minutes tinkering with the placement of the meat.

"Three more centimeters to the left – you want to be two inches away from that coal."

"Dad, can we stick to one standard of measurement? Going from standard to metric seems unnecessarily complicated."

Wait, flip, tinker, and repeat until we – through a mind meld with the rapidly warming flesh of a dead animal – achieve a nice medium. Those sizzlers will get tossed onto a plate where they will sit, stewing in their own juices for a few minutes. After they have stewed, one of us will deliver a mighty chop with an obnoxiously large knife to see if we got the temperatures we desired.

In this instance, the grilling went off as planned. U.S. government meteorological satellites likely picked up the fireball, possibly causing a spike in the average global temperature for a second. (Seriously, NOAA should know by now that any temperate anomaly in Central MD is caused by me lighting a grill.)

24

Meat was placed on the rack. Severe burns were avoided. The meat was a little north of medium, but that is mostly my fault for being too cautious. Nothing will stunt the growth of a new griller like sending his family to the emergency room with searing stomach pain due to raw or undercooked meat. (Fun fact: my wife and I spent her first Mother's Day in the emergency room. Some part of the previous night's BBQ - cooked by someone else; not me - did not agree with us and tried – successfully – to eject itself with haste. For hours.)

Everyone involved knows that this is not the end of the road. Instead, it is Mile Marker 1 on a trail that will take a lifetime to complete. There are more cuts of meat to master, each with its own idiosyncrasies, dozens of techniques, and years to conquer the pairing of meats (and sides) with beverages. It is up to the head griller to get this all in line before handing things off to the dessert fiends, a unique breed all to themselves.

I will still have to teach Oldest how to shoot, so he can independently acquire grillable meat without having to kowtow to the meat packing industry. This will be tough. I am not very good at shooting things, and I don't particularly like shooting things. The last time I went hunting for bear – I hear their meat goes well with a…wait for it…nice bearnaise sauce – the bear got tired of all my misses and gave me a few pointers in a charming Canadian accent. In

25

return, I promised not to shoot him. Spoiler alert: 1) he was a good teacher and 2) he was delicious.

I know my job is not done, there is much more in life that a father needs to teach his kids. I still must teach them how to pay a mechanic to do basic auto repair tasks – changing windshield wiper blades, for example - that could easily be handled at home for a fraction of the cost, among other things. For now, however, I can take pride in knowing that I have successfully moved the ball forward a few yards in the Father's Quest of teaching life lessons. It is a worthy quest. Even something so simple as hosting a cookout can lead to meaningful human interaction.

Re-learning How to Swear

"There ought to be a room in every house to swear in. It's dangerous to have to repress an emotion like that." - Mark Twain

Swearing while trying to be creative, dammit.

I am trying to be a writer. Writing, on its face, is easy. If you have a basic understanding of your native language, you can usually vomit out a few words that are somewhat coherent. They might not be good, but "me use good words a lot" is, technically, writing. If you can get words on a page, or a computer, or tablet, or smartphone, or even etched into a slab of granite, you have written.

Hell, it still kind of counts if you can pee your name into fresh-fallen snow. It counts as high-brow humor if you pee "free lemon-flavored snowballs!" into the snow.

I like to think that I have moved past the examples above, but I know that I am by no means good. Writing is a lifelong pursuit, and I can always improve. That is not why I swear with increasing frequency these days. Writing, in and of itself is not enough on its own to get those juices flowing. In my old career, I was an accomplished writer of reports and analytic pieces. Here on the outside, that is not good enough. Now, to get people to read what I write, I must do so much more than simply commit words to a "Word" document. These additional steps are alien to my corporate world mentality and have led to the uptick in swearing.

Technology

I am authoring a novel about millionaire amateur base jumpers who get snared in conifers and eaten by bears. (That is not a joke.) It is a lengthy process, as you fellow writers know, and I started writing short, stupid stuff as that novel effort plods along. I started with a personal blog and have since branched out to other platforms, which has increased my ability to write more often.

Sometimes, I even write when I am not sitting on the can.

Setting up my personal site was its own hot mess. Even the Amish are more internet savvy than I am. (I did manage to score an address with proper spelling conventions. No www.br3!!c4r3s!.com here.) I'm still trying to figure out how to use widgets — I thought Widget was a character in a 1980's era spin-off from Star Wars. Getting the widgets to display properly, in an appealing order, has been tough.

"I just wanted to include an 'add comment' section. Why is there an ad for the Red Lobster location in Omaha, Nebraska on my page now?"

In time, I think, I managed to create a site that will not sear your eyeballs or tempt you to go to Lobsterfest. (If you want to go to

Lobsterfest, go nuts — I am not judging. That is just not really the point of my website.)

Enter the wife

I am not sure if my wife wanted to help, or torment, by recommending that I expand to other sites. She had good reason for both motivations — we are married and love each other. But goodness knows I have been known to torment her. I once argued, with my extremely health-conscious wife, that I was not going to eat vegetables anymore because I eat cows. Cows eat vegetables. Two birds, one stone. No more vegetables, and I would be just as healthy!

"Instagram would be fun — you could take neat pictures," she said, "and add neat quotes about birds and nature! You just have to use your cell phone."

My phone is older than former President Dwight D. Eisenhower and has a crack in the screen that is so deep that — if the lighting is right — you can see straight into the depths of Hell. So, I had to set up an account on one (of our two) laptops, take a picture using my broke-ass phone, email it to myself, use a free app to make it pretty and…who knows what else. By the time Instagram was telling me to go f---myself (the swearing goes both directions) by displaying my images upside down, I stopped cataloging the process.

Eventually, I figured it out (but only after asking Instagram what its f---ing problem was, and why the s--- it hates me so much). However, at the start, the kids would drop whatever they were doing when they sensed that Dad was trying something new and rush into the room. They are fond of my word constructs. Mercifully, they have yet to repeat them outside of the house.

Seriously, they were on the verge of perfecting a nuclear fusion reactor, possibly ensuring generational wealth for our family, before I distracted them by trying to post a picture of a duck taking a dump.

Trying to get published

There is a button at the top right part of my screen — as I type this sentence — that says "publish". At any moment, I could click it, and publish this drivel. But no one would ever read it. Writing and publishing are just a fraction of the game. There is something called SEO — Search Engine Optimization — that is really nothing more than trying to convince a bunch of computers that you exist. It is a rather heartless, but necessary process. Computers are very fickle about what I need to demonstrate before they even acknowledge I am a human and not another computer. I must type intentionally distorted letters as I see them. Sometimes, I must click on all the pictures that have busses running over lemurs in the shot. It is also maddening (the "verify that you are a human" thing is creative, however) – all of this is before I even start to use nifty sounding codes (key phrase! Hash tag! Etc.) to let computers know the content of my writing to let other like-minded people find it.

Yesterday, "#dadblogger" was a good thing. Today it links my work to a documentary on serial killers.

Tagging, URL slugs, key phrases (whatever the f--- these things are), and SEO snippets are key to getting seen. That is before we even get to the pictures. Pictures that have to be underneath the sub headline that falls under the main headline.

Alt-image

After weeks of floundering in the new universe of compu-bulls*&^ that my wife suckered me into, I found a plugin that would, ostensibly, help me with my SEO rating of -1.6 trillion. The automated nagger prodded me to start adding "alt image" information that would help other automated naggers find my post. (Note: it wasn't until the last steps of editing that

I found out what "alt image" was designed for. I apologize to any confused blind people who have read previous articles by me!)

It is a picture of a grill. If you want me to add text to attract viewers, I will just tack on "hot nudes" to the "alt image" for every image that I insert.

Sure, there will never be hot nudes on my page, but hey, if you click on it, I still get a "view", which helps my SEO. Swish.

Of course, there is also guidance out there that suggests you limit the number of images you use. I guess this distracts the reader. Only post one pic of kittens playing with yarn, alt-imaged with "sweet asses" (you do not want to go to the "hot nudes" well too often).

Nearing the end

At this point, I had used a creative process to write something that I thought was worth reading. I did not have to swear at that part, even though the "g" key on my keyboard gets stuck. After that, I tried to sucker the internet into reading my content by promising the opportunity to see hot nudes.

There are no nudes in this post. #hotnudes

With that, 15 more views.

Swearing at the Office

While swearing at things was not an integral part of the writing process at my old office zombie job, it sure was part of everyday life there. I didn't really swear in college. I had finally learned that using an expletive is meant for emphasis. Using four letter words in a sentence "just for fun" watered down the impact significantly. Ironically, when I got a job as a professional with the Federal government, it became a necessity to understand and utilize superfluous swearing, just like my middle school days. When I learned these words at Bel Air Middle School, I used them with an alarming — and nonsensical — frequency.

"F--- this textbook!"

What the hell does that mean? It sounds like a command to a friend to have sexual intercourse with a history book on Mesopotamia. That situation, if properly executed, would be very bad for everyone involved. Not to put too fine a point on it, but there would be several injured parties.

Nonetheless, after a brief retirement from swearing just to swear, life in the office brought it all back to life. It is like riding a bike, to borrow a hack simile. Typically, after returning

34

to my desk, someone would ask "How the f---
are you?". Well, Hank, I just took a dump. I'm
not entirely sure why the f-word was needed, but
I guess I'm feeling pretty good. Those baby back
ribs that I had for breakfast were laying kind of
heavy, so I am happy to have freed up some
intestinal real estate. If that is "f---ing good", I
feel "f---ing great"!

At first, it seemed like a minor cultural
difference that could easily be overcome. The
English language is pretty versatile. I figured
there could be some leeway in office chatter
diction. I was mistaken. Even though "crap",
"dump", and "s---" are all four-letter words that
describe the exact same thing, I became an
outsider for eschewing the last word on that list.

I was fearful that my use of the English
language would hinder my promotional
opportunities. For the first several months, I
simply could not add "f---ing" into a sentence
about coffee.

*"This coffee is f---ing terrible." Possibly, but
how/why is coffee "f---ing" someone named
Terrible? Also, this is the same coffee that Hank
made yesterday. The status of its quality -
assuming that is what you were referencing -
ought not be news."*

It became increasingly clear that my performance review would read something like this:

"Mr. Chrest adequately contributed to the office's long-term mission by using complex sentences to refute Hank's argument in favor of microwaving salmon in the office. However, he could have saved us precious seconds by simply stating 'this is bulls---'. If he was a f---ing team player and talked like the rest of us f---ers, he would have gotten a f---ing raise. As is, D f---ing plus."

So, I re-learned how to step up to the goddamn plate and swing the f---ing bat.

Fast forward to last night.

After 15+ years in that environment, old habits die hard. My wife and I were having a delightfully deep conversation on philosophy with some friends. We discussed David Hume, Stephen Hawking, and a whole host of other topics. In time, we got to a subject on which my wife and I — respectfully — disagree on: whether or not King Victor Amadeus III of Sardinia was truly conservative, or just espoused some leanings in that direction by coincidence. After she laid out her argument over the course of 5 minutes, laced with intelligent thoughts (the King did declare war on Revolutionary France in

1792) that were devoid of logical fallacies, I made my rebuttal.

"That's bulls---."

Stay-at-Home Daddying

"If the past cannot teach the present, and
the father cannot teach the son, then
history need not have bothered to go on,
and the world has wasted a great deal of
time." - Russell Hoban

Several years ago, my wife and I hatched a plan for me to pause my career and be a stay-at-home dad for up to three years. She had been a stay-at-home mom since giving birth to our first child and was set to resume her career. She was not making what I was (different industries) but we had been aggressively saving for some time. I went about a year staying at home before a wonderful opportunity to pursue my dream career arrived. Still, as a working-again-dad, I think it is worth reflecting on my time at home with two young boys. There were a lot of changes to all our routines, and a lot of lessons to be learned. Going from 15+ years of wearing a suit every day to wearing the same pair of sweatpants three days in a row is quite the change-up. Note: underwear and t-shirts were constantly cycling, however.

My old world was fond of etched-in-granite schedules and full slates of meetings. Whether it was a Skype call with satellite offices, a superfluous in-person meeting about nothing relevant, or mandatory fun events, there was always something. And for every meeting, there were 2-3 people who would send out email invites – especially if the point of the meeting was mandatory fun.

"It's Waffle Wednesday! Let's go burn two hours of time to get waffles!"

"I don't like waffles."

"Come and get a f–king waffle, ass."

I don't intend to paint my office with the proverbial broad brush – most supervisors and coworkers eschewed meaningless meetings – but, as in all workplaces, we did have a special cadre of people who just wanted to talk. A lot. And to make matters worse, they knew how to sucker us into attending.

I had one meeting in which someone went on for more than 15 minutes about an article they had read online. It was about how foreign investment in the U.S. film industry could present an "issue". It was unclear what that "issue" was, and God knows the movie industry had nothing to do with our mission set, but if you see a trailer for "Fast and Furious 18: Sacre Bleu!", I guess my coworker - or at least the author of the article - was onto something and right to call out the French.

Time to break the schedule cycle

During my stint as a stay-at-home dad, which coincided with the COVID pandemic, we kept the boys on a loose, but consistent, schedule. For most of the morning, and again for an hour or so in the afternoon, my wife – a teacher – is in her office conducting distance teaching stuff. So, I handle the lion's share of the boys' educational regimen. We will do some schoolwork, take a fun break, and then get back to the book learning' stuff until lunch. It is going great! I am a master educator. Kind of.

The boys and I like to play an Xbox1 NASCAR game. One day, my wife was teaching, and we were playing this game during a break. Something odd happened to me (I was actually playing for real for once, and not just driving in the wrong direction to run into oncoming traffic).

Me: "Bulls–t. No way that crash would send me in some random ass direction."

Some 30 minutes later, my wife came up to take a break and see how we are doing.

Wife: "How's it going guys?"

Oldest: "Daddy's car went in a random ass direction."

Youngest: "It was bulls–t."

Like I said, master educator. In fairness to me, that is a rare slip up re: the old' salty language. Also, Youngest properly drew out the "bull" part. It was "bullllllllllllllllsh" – you get the idea.

No meetings, a looser schedule, and some fun piled on top of academics. I call that a win.

Exercise and workplace sweat

For the last six years of my career, I worked on a campus that was laid out in such a manner that all related offices were – in some cases, literally – as far apart from each other as physically possible. As a result, I would find myself walking 2-3 miles a day. This was great for cardio, especially since there is some arcane Federal rule that mandates meetings must start less than 10 minutes after the previous meeting, regardless of the distance that needs to be covered to make it to the next conference room.

I sweat a lot, and in winter, when the heat was jacked up, this extra cardio became an issue. Sweating is something I am really good at and having to hustle 4.8km to a meeting exacerbates that condition. One time a coworker came up to me after a meeting and inquired:

Coworker: "Why do you like sitting back in the corner?"

Me: "Want to feel my armpits? Cuz any moisture issues you find there are 20 times worse south of the border. Picking up what I'm putting down?"

Coworker: "Proper."

At home, I walk less. I love running around with the boys outside, but I do not think that adds up to the same distances I was covering as an office worker (which sounds strange). The type of cardio is different as well. In the office, endurance had more value than at home. Home-running requires short bursts of speed, like when a kid is blindly chasing an errant ball into the street. I do, however, lift more weights and do more push-ups and whatnot. This is a double-edged sword: increased strength makes picking up big objects more feasible, but decreased cardio means I need to measure my rate of unnecessarily dicking with gravity for fear of a heart attack.

The Great Outdoors

I have started going outside by myself, even traveling 20 yards to sit on a bench in our garden to get devoured by mosquitoes in the vainglorious hope that looking at all the mulch I broke my back to spread will give me some return on investment. My wife and I have always enjoyed being outdoors with the boys. We like to play football, soccer, go for walks, and supervise the grueling yard work tasks that we assign to them. Basically, we watch as they try to squirt each other with a hose in the hopes that a few droplets will incidentally hit the garden. When we are outside though, we are a herd. Herds protect members from predators (which led to my fear of venturing into the wild solo). The only time a member of the herd is really at risk, is when they wander off...

I have seen those shows on National Geographic about African wildlife. Inevitably, some dull antelope decides to check out a Zambian coin someone on safari must have dropped.

*"Wow! That is 50 ngwee! Even though I have no
need to use human currency, I will temporarily
leave the herd. I can catch up."*

*"You silly sod," I yell at the TV. "You should
only risk your life for a full kwacha coin!"*

As soon as Arthur the Antelope trots off,
the lions pounce. The footage is unnecessarily
graphic. I had no idea that those 'lopes had so
many internal organs — why do you need six
lungs? As such, I was perpetually terrified that a
pride of domesticated felines would strike as
soon as I get far enough away from the other
humans. But at least I would got my Vitamin D,
and that seems beneficial if you believe the
internet.

Food consumption

Staying with health and diet, my food
consumption is pretty much the same. I have not
really changed much here, and I still have a
weird feeding schedule – starting lunch at
10:00AM or so and nibbling all the way to
3:00PM. When I was in the office, my coworkers
found my habits to be pretty amusing. Since I
would have leftover carry-out for lunch once or
twice a week, they'd see me noshing on
refrigerated leftover ribs/wings/Chinese
food/Japanese sea urchin that had been over-
nighted to our house the previous day, etc., long
before most people had finished their coffee. My
email nickname became Breakfast_Ribs.

To this day, I befuddle my wife by having nacho cheese and pretzels and/or tortilla chips before the brunching hour. I am a man without a ton of hankering' control. If I want to eat something in particular, and it is in the house, your boy is going to crush it.

I recall the look on my kids' faces when they first saw me eating leftover General Tso's chicken at 10:06AM. At the same time, I find toaster strudels to be perfectly acceptable dinner food. Lunch can be anything from half a can of Pringles to a fruit salad (of course along with the now room temperature holdovers from General Tso's chicken army).

The joys of daytime television

Whereas food stuff really has not changed, my TV viewing/internet use sure did. In the office, I had extremely limited access to the internet or cable news. When I got home for the day, I only had a narrow slice of time to ingest the news of the day, forcing me to be brutally efficient in terms of what I read. Now, I can have cable news on in the background all day if I want…this was a curse.

I cannot tell you how many times I watched the same canned segment 5+ times while the kids were "in school". Admittedly, this is a self-inflicted wound, and – in fairness to me – I can be productive while it is on. Still, for some reason, I cannot turn the news off for any protracted length of time. So, at the top of the hour at 7:00PM, I would see the same exact segment that I watched at 11:00AM. And eight hours since it first aired, BREAKING NEWS would still be in the chyron.

Suckering me into clicking links to stories I don't care about

We have all clicked on a news/sports/entertainment story from a website and seen all the "sponsored content" ads at the end, rife with click-bait headlines. When I was working, I did not have enough time to click on "25 Ways Tom Cruise Avoids Toenail Fungus," which was sponsored by www.funwithfungus.com. All these ads are delightfully formulaic. It starts with a headline like "10 Ways to Save Money that Wall Street Does NOT Want You to Know About." This sets up an adversarial situation in which the reader is prone to think "Those jerks! I'll show them! I'll click on this RIGHT NOW!"

Then, after 10+ pages of ads, the reader is treated to a "tip" about not using high interest credit cards and to make a mortgage payment more than twice a year. I suppose the big nasties on Wall Street do not want the commoner to have good credit, but I doubt that they are having high level meetings in 87th floor boardrooms about the topic.

That is not all. Some sponsored content likes to inform the public about neat facts about pop culture fads. I had all kinds of time to learn about such fantastic things, things in the "real world" that I was blind to while working in an office. Did you know that Chewbacca needs 14 cruise ship quality towels to dry off after a shower (from "10 Ways the Cast Stayed Comfortable When Filming Star Wars")? That the 1976 New York Knicks had an extraterrestrial point guard? It's true - I read it in an "article" called "Crazy but True Stories About Athletes"! I cannot believe how much I have learned since March. If you need a reason to quit your job, this is it.

On the downside, daytime TV commercials taught me a lot about potential signs of fatal diseases that their product — for just $500 dollars a pill! — can cure. I have been a hypochondriac since as long as I can remember, and I have had more psychosomatic ailments than most everyone. In June of 1987, for instance, I was convinced that I had gill cancer.

I had to create a database that correlates "sign" to "disease". If I get a small reddish bump on my nose, is it malaria? Or toe cancer? I am not trying to play roulette with my health. Each of these horrifying diseases have multiple symptoms and I — an untrained medical professional — need to properly self-diagnose.

Lord of the Showers

When I was working in an office I would shower when I woke up. Then, after I got home, I would shower again and change out of my suit. This was mostly to make it tolerable for my wife to be near me, but it also served to get out of the damn suit. Over time, I got very comfortable wearing a suit on the Metro, while sitting at my desk and even when praying for an evacuation drill while mired in an interminable meeting. I never got the hang of lounging in a suit, however. Maybe I would have been more successful if I had tried harder, but hindsight being 20/20 and all that...

After dinner, I would work out a bit. This was no great endeavor – just 20-30 minutes of physical activity. But keep this in mind: activities such as eye-blinking, heart-pumping, and breathing are enough to make me sweat. Real workouts, even the shorter ones, have me roaming the streets looking for a hydrating IV. I would be drenched by the time I had finished stretching (even if it was a freezing day and I wasn't wearing a shirt). Before bed, I would shower again. If I did not shower, our bed sheets would have to be handled by a specially trained HAZMAT team just to get them to our washer. Neighbors would have to be evacuated.

While staying-at-home? Who cares? As long as I do not let my skin get so bad it sloughs

off, I pretty much have a free hand in
determining if/when I shower. I'll typically punt
on the morning shower and then wait until I
work out — or until my wife complains — and
mop off then. Our water bill has gone down
precipitously. Some days, like "weekdays", I
rarely even shower at all. Really, what's the
point? I start sweating when I pick up the towel
to dry off after shower, negating any progress I
may have made over the last 10 minutes.

*"Just air dry. There's no need to get us involved
in this train wreck." — My towels.*

I went months without even putting on
deodorant starting March 13, 2020. That is not
an arbitrary date — it was my last day in the
office. You wouldn't believe how much money I
have saved by not buying deodorant. If I ever
write a book of life hacks, there will be a chapter
called "How to Afford a Dream Disney World
Vacation just by Eliminating Body Wash and
Deodorant". It will be a short chapter, since I
pretty much gave everything away in the title.

And, if I am being honest, I am still
wearing the same pair of undershorts I wore to
play tennis yesterday. At least they are moisture
wicking.

You can understand why May's nice
weather and open windows became a very
positive development for our family (especially
the cats). Even if our property abutted a

slaughterhouse/sausage making complex, open windows would be a huge improvement.

The curse of the cell phone

While working, I never answered my cell phone during the day. I could not. We were not allowed to have cell phones in my office. The only time we were allotted or "were allowed" to check our phones was when we went to the bathroom and could pick them up from a lockbox on the way to the toilet. Even then, there was usually only time (unless something went horribly wrong in your GI tract) to check Facebook and Twitter (this still took the better part of an hour). Now, since I am at home, when a random telephone number calls, I cheerfully answer "Hello!" It started mostly as a morbid curiosity but devolved into more of a habit. This is a terrible routine, and one that I hope to break.

Caller: "Hi! This is Trying-Piss-You-Off Life insurance (TPYOLI). We have the lowest rates out there! To get started, I just need to know your age. Feel free to toss in your social security number and checking account routing number if you like."

Me: "I already have life insurance that I am happy with."

Caller: "Can I just have your age?"

Me: "Forsooth, I was born four score and seven years ago."

Caller: <hangs up>

I have gotten better of late, but the little imp in me still likes to have fun with the more egregious/unbelievable calls. I know it is not the caller's fault, per se, and I sincerely hope that I have livened up a few of their days.

"Look bud, I am happy that I qualify for a free cruise to Tahiti, but I just ate a burrito that has been sitting out all night and the only trip that I'm taking right now is a trip to Pooptown and you aren't invited."

<hangs up>

My new fortress of solitude

Speaking of Pooptown...when I was working, I still had to poop. I just took a lot longer to get the job done. I no longer had to use the stall to double as a cone of silence, blocking any office-related noise aside from the occasional grunt of despair or sigh of relief. I was afforded a safe haven there, devoid of the banalities of office conversation.

"Can you believe how hot it is out there?"

"Yes. I can. I had to go outside to get here just like you did, and the temperature is an objective measure that does not require a leap of faith to 'believe' in it. This is not witchcraft – it is simply measuring mercury in a glass tube."

51

Now, with full access to the internet outside of the can, I have all the motivation in the world to wrap up a task that takes 5–10 minutes in 5–10 minutes and not in 40–45 minutes. Dropping a deuce used to be a gateway to the free world (well, the free world of social media, anyway). Now, it is just a hindrance that gets in the way of being able to watch the same Bulls-Lakers highlights on ESPN that I have already seen three times. Or, given my fondness for perpetual nibbling, getting a head start on starting the whole digestive process over again.

Holy cow, did I miss <important event>?

Checking the calendar is something that I never really had to do while working. Thanks to the Outlook calendar junkies in the office, I knew everything that was going to happen. Usually, I'd first be aware of it months in advance, and then receive follow up reminders weekly or daily. We even had one person who would put all of our parents, spouses, and kids' birthdays into the Outlook calendar. Of course, they did not tailor the distro, so everyone knew everyone else's significant dates. The scheme fell apart when people (like me) would respond to data calls for dates with stuff like "July 13th, anniversary of Uncle Luke's severed arm accident".

At home, unless I googled "calendar", I generally had no idea what date it was since weekends were no longer distinct from weekdays. In August, I had a moment of calendar panic. I knew my wife's birthday, and I knew it fell on a Friday this year — BUT WHAT IF I ALREADY MISSED IT? Fridays were not distinguishable from other days that end in" y" and August is like any other summer month in Maryland: hot, humid, chance of PM thunderstorms. My wife is nice enough to ignore such slights, but I try not to go to that well as much as possible, especially since I had enough time in my day to argue with a telephone solicitor regarding the moral implications of extended warranties. So, I fled to the laptop, fired up Google and…. Safe. According to two reputable websites, I had not missed her special day. But that took a lot of sweat and work, so...

...now, I make it a point to check the print calendar that someone, possibly one of the cats, affixed to the side of the refrigerator. I had no idea it was there, even though since we were now in August, I suspect was present for at least eight months. It is a very effective tool despite being super-low tech. It doesn't have a charger and yet it can still accurately predict which day of the week Friday the 13th falls on! I have no idea who thought of this, but he makes Steve Jobs look like a chump. I am pretty sure that we had our wedding anniversary coming up; I seemed to recall that it is in one of the –er months. I really hoped to get this routine set in stone so I can have more anniversaries.

I was already on thin ice after the time I forgot we had two kids, and not just one. Please note that it was just a verbal screw up. I orally referenced "our kid", implying that we only had one child. I did not strap a kid into the car seat in the Target parking lot and drive off leaving the other son standing on the curb clutching the new Lego pirate ship set he just got.

The Family Life

Speaking of family life, that was so much nicer. During the times when I should have been showering but wasn't, I was thinking – since I knew I'd eventually go back to work – about how to maximize all of these special times when things got busy. On any given day, my kids would have: 1) proudly shown me several math/science/reading assignments that they had completed; 2) shown off their artwork and/or whatever they had learned from their German lesson du jour (that's not a joke – they were learning German. Das est gut!); 3) possibly made fun of me in German; 4) asked me (in English) to play with them.

As if I would ever turn that down.

My wife was happier as well – I was an incorrigible asshole far less often than I showered (and I was certainly not showering often), even reaching streaks of non-assholery that would last weeks. Something about not having to deal with a coworker's obsession with the film industry seemed to calm my nerves and helped to put things in perspective.

Another life review

So, on it went and as getting a new job edged closer and closer, I gave myself another review. There is no point in not taking time to learn from the experience, even the trivial things. As of March 13, 2020, all of these things – and many more - stopped doing themselves for some reason.

For example:

Grocery shopping: I am familiar enough with the entire process now that I feel qualified to complain about things like store layout, self-checkout no-nos, and improper cart usage/storage. A quick note about store layout: I love seeing commercials like "Try new Farmer Ray's all organic turnips! Look for it in your grocer's astringent chemical aisle." I know what that aisle has now, Ray. You can't fool me – there's nothing organic that makes it onto that shelf space.

Laundry: I had a streak of several weeks where I did not screw up the settings (mostly because I did not change them, and my wife did not notice). My streak came to a halt when we had to get a new washer and I accidently selected "pre-wash with itching powder". C'est la vie.

Vacuuming: It sucks. For every three pieces of dirt it picks up, it drops around 57. I have no idea where it gets all that dirt from, but it looks like a river of Legos after I try to vacuum up the remains of Lego Gettysburg.

Being a house human instead of an office zombie continued to be a very interesting trip. At first, I noticed the major things. For example, the laundry stopped folding itself. Meals needed to be prepared, sometimes through the employment of multiple steps. After clearing those major hurdles (I was no longer intimidated by microwave meals that required "stir, replace cover and continue heating for 3-3.5 minutes"), I began to take stock of the more subtle changes. Starting with the large and then refining down to the small was useful. Even if it was for silly stuff, the whole exercise provided a valuable template for re-application in other areas.

Back into the Classroom

"Tell me and I'll forget. Show me, and I may not remember. Involve me, and I'll understand." - Native American Proverb

For about as long as I have been considering realistic career goals (that is, not being the starting second baseman for the Baltimore Orioles), "teacher" was on the short list along with "engineer", "intelligence analyst", and "dune buggy driver". After a series of amusing events after I graduated college, I settled on "teacher". It turns out, however, that school systems prefer people with teaching degrees and not degrees that are focused on international relations, especially ones on Russia after the fall of Communism. I put that on hold and joined the Federal Bureau of Investigation as an analyst.

Originally, "engineer" was the top choice, but by October of my first semester I had learned that one does not just become an engineer. One has to know math, physics, and why jet airliners are not made out of super glue and balsa wood. I was out of the running.

I was in the FBI for 15+ years. The job was an excellent job for a while but grew stale – through no one's fault – over time. I figured I was stuck – nowhere closer to a degree in education than I was a decade and a half ago – and was kind of resolved to my fate. But my loving wife hatched a plan and on March 13, 2020, I walked out of my FBI office for the last time.

That also, unexpectedly, was the day that everything shut down due to COVID. We had planned on me being a stay-at-home dad for a while in between jobs, but this confirmed it. With the horse out of the barn, I had a lot of time to think.

Did I even know how to teach? Was this like engineering, where you actually needed to know basic skills?

Also, I started to think about what I was like as a student in grade school, and how students (my wife is a teacher) had evolved over time. When I was in school, we'd do wacky stuff like all drop our pencils at some pre-appointed time. Or throw wads of paper at each other when the hapless teacher wasn't looking. Now, kids were stealing cars.

That's not a joke. Some of my wife's students actually stole her car. She left her keys on her desk to fill up her water bottle and then – pow! – the keys, some kids, and her car were gone. I was in St. Louis on business at the time. My wife called when I was walking west on Market St., after visiting the Gateway Arch while killing time until my flight.

"Hi sweetheart, how are you?"

"I might not be able to pick you up from the airport tonight. Some students stole my car."

"Heh, good one! Anyhow, I'll see you around nine. Love yo..."

"No – seriously. I'll call you back when I know more."

...u."

In the end, she was able to borrow her dad's pickup truck (which I think was used in WWII given how old it looked) and pick me up. All's well that ends well, but the flashing "explosion imminent" light next to the "check engine light" was not very reassuring.

My first thought was to counter this escalation by going full "old man" on the first day:

"There's nothing you got that I haven't seen before! I was smuggling portable CD players into class so I could listen to Pearl Jam when you were just a twinkle in your Momma's eye!"

That, on closer inspection, did not seem practical since, regardless of whatever grade I was assigned, every student there would have a cell phone equipped with technology I had never seen before.

After that idea fell flat on its face, I considered relying on my background in philosophy. Vivacious discussions on the role of education in a republic and the formation of equitable laws had to be of universal interest, right? No dice. It didn't take long for me to realize that I didn't even care enough about the Hegelian Dialectic to talk about it for longer than a commercial break during Monday Night Football.

Was I a lunatic for signing up for this, even with the promise of a Fall/Thanksgiving break, a Winter/Christmas Break, a Spring/Easter Break, and a Summer/Blueberry Day (July 8) break? How did normal people do this? Sure – my wife is a teacher, but she is far from normal. Just look at the kook she married. As COVID settled in, it was clear that we weren't going "back to normal" anytime soon.

I began to consider some options. Working at Denny's seemed appealing. They were never busy, and I could test out the deep fryer on household items like a clothes iron, or a G.I. Joe toy, or even a plush Garfield. A bookstore wouldn't be so bad. I like books – I am planning to write one – and could help customers out quite a bit.

"No ma'am, I think Stephen King's 'It' would be perfect for your 11-year-old. Especially if Billy likes clowns as much as you say he does!"

As long as I wore a fake name tag, not even Yelp! could take me down.

"This seems like a great bookstore based on its reviews! We just have to stay away from a sales associate named M. C. Hammer."

A chance to meet other teachers

As luck would have it, as I drifted further into despair, I was afforded the chance to meet some of my wife's teaching co-workers.

One night a few months after the start of the COVID pandemic, my family was invited to spend some time together with a bunch of math teachers that my wife worked with. Her math department had their end-of-year cookout, and I was the +1. I know that my wife was hoping I would decline the invitation so she could take the hunky French guy from Nantes that lives down the street and pretend that he was me.

No dice. I've been known to enjoy a good cookout. Even if it meant chilling with a gaggle of math teachers, I was not going to pass up the chance to sample someone else's 'que. That's not to judge, but to learn. Everyone adds their own flair to the process.

I had no idea what to expect. I know a math teacher, obviously, and as previously discussed, she is not normal. Aside from marrying me, she doesn't like pro-wrestling or hoppy beers. She likes to run and do yoga. She only eats meat on one randomly selected day every month that starts with A or M. She would rather read a historical fiction romance novel than wait for the movie to see Michael Bay's interpretation.

We arrived fashionably late — that is not by design. It is just the reality of life with two kids in tow. I met six math teachers. They seemed pretty normal, but I was still wary: the array of wine, beer, and liquor followed the rules of a right triangle, per the Pythagorean Theorem.

"No! You cannot take that beer! It will upset the ratio of side A to side B! Wait for someone to take that wine cooler first!"

One even referred to a patty as an "irregular cylinder". In my mind, an "irregular cylinder" means you are not getting all your engine's horsepower and need to see a mechanic.

Nonetheless, there had to be some normal in them — after all, they did choose to mingle with others outside of work.

Everyone was fun to be around, affable, and — though I am no psychologist — sane. Seriously, they like math, and approximately 180 days a year, subject themselves to verbal abuse from teenagers. Their sanity was a valid question, and I did not feel guilty about mentally conducting basic assessments.

The only odd thing was when the one big guy started wearing his sunglasses backwards. It was as if he was trying to protect some of his hair from whatever UV rays the sun had remaining for the fading day. Nice guy though — and he has two very UV protected ovals on the back of his head.

We joked, laughed, and talked about normal people stuff. We even ate normally shaped food, even though all of the food had math shape related names. It took me a few minutes to figure out that a "truncated cone half-filled with NaCl" was a saltshaker. No calculations were required, but there was a touch of a language barrier.

Our kids, in addition to two other children who seemed perfectly normal, somehow acquired croquet mallets. They spent their time clubbing any clubbable object in the host's yard. There were lots of clubbable objects that the mallets were not designed to club, and I was happy that the impulse to club them – a very normal emotional response – carried the day.

The next time the hosts try to play croquet, I predict that a lot of balls are going to go in a random direction, possibly causing them to make standard deviation graphs or whatever.

The group spent plenty of time yakking it up, asking about summer plans, and talking about next year. They had just finished the first academic season with COVID and had every excuse to run as far away from teaching as possible. Yet, there they were, over well-done irregular cylinders chatting about the year to come in a meaningful way. In the middle of light-hearted banter, a faculty meeting would break out for a few minutes. While my focus was making sure that the only objects getting clubbed by croquet mallets were inanimate objects – like garden gnomes – and not, for example, frogs, the teachers were sharing best practices and whatnot.

The faculty meeting would run its course and the conversation would turn back to topics like shockingly tawdry bachelor/bachelorette parties and the like. I resisted the urge to take a break in conversation to joke:

"I've just recorded the last 10 minutes of your conversation on my phone. If you do not want this posted to your class's webpage, well...checks can be made out to..."

It was inspiring, to say the least. At the time, only God knew if/when our children would have a more normal next academic year. At least I know that there is a cadre of professional educators that are going to do their best to make the best of a sad situation.

That is how they roll, I guess. Or, perhaps more accurately, that is how they vector.

If you are wondering how I managed to remain relevant, I ate plenty of food and made several poop jokes. I guess that is another lesson as to the power of the suburban BBQ: everyone is welcome, even if they have no idea what a dodecahedron is. Nonetheless, I could not shake the feeling that at least one faculty member stayed home to devise a new algorithm for even more efficient/cost effective means to acquire quinoa.

Fitness Part I – Individual Efforts/Sports

"Surely a person of sense would submit to anything, like exercise, so as to obtain a well-functioning mind and a pleasant, happy life." - Socrates

Soccer

I played rec league soccer when I was a kid. It was the league without (many) bulging nerves in the faces of the coaches. We still had juice and orange wedges at halftime. Win or lose, a trip to McDonald's for McIce Cream was in the McCards.

In lieu of hyper-complex formations with wingbacks, holding midfields, and false 9s, we played a 1-6-3-3 formation. You might be thinking: "wait - that is 13 players. Isn't 11 the maximum?" You are right. But we figured out there was some wiggle room since there were only two coaches and, most importantly, one referee. I think we got up to 15 players on the field at one time before someone finally called shenanigans. I'll never forget inching away from the coach and then – just as the referee had his back turned to follow a pack of players – sneaking onto the field.

I might have felt bad if the other team was not doing it as well. Even at that age, we could all appreciate how funny it was for our 15th player to be off in some corner of the field talking to their #14.

The best games were the rainy-day games. Not only could we play outside in the rain, but we forced our stodgy parents to be outside as well.

As the parents muttered hateful things towards God under their breath, we would slosh around, making the most out of our time in front of either goal. That was the territory that had long since lost its turf and was nothing more than a conglomeration of mud hills and mud puddles. If the run of play dictated that we had to traverse the parts of the field that somehow retained its grass, we would go to great measures to superfluously slide, since the moist surface allowed for ridiculous distances to be traveled.

One field in particular – at Ring Factory Elementary School - was especially amazing: for some reason, the county did not bother to grade the pitch. As such, the halfway line was a solid ten feet higher in elevation than one of the goal lines. That entire half of the field played downhill at a considerable rate of change. If you were headed in that direction, you slid. That was a fact. And no other player would give you a hard time about it.

Coach: "What are you doing?! You had the ball, an open goal…and you just slid? Why didn't you shoot? Scoring goals is a relatively important facet of this sport!"

Player 1: <shrugs>

Players 2-15: <high five> "Proper."

We were not very good most seasons. For ten
weekends a fall, we would travel around the
county giving up goals and getting in some
wicked good sliding. Sometimes, another player
got in the way, upgrading the slide to a slide
tackle.

Our best chance at winning came when
the opposing team's local McDonald's had a bad
week in food handling and the better part of their
starting lineup had been wracked with e. coli
related issues. Nonetheless, those years were
great years, and I would not trade them for
anything (that is not entirely true – I would trade
them for a solid gold 19′ statue of myself in
underpants that could be erected on my front
lawn). Most games were fun and, even if we lost,
it was well in the rearview mirror by the time we
got to the parking lot.

There were only two games that ended
with a less than pleasant feeling. For the first, it
was, for lack of a better word, "bad". As in
physically bad. I had lost more than a game, I
had lost feeling in my toes. For the second game,
I – again – lost more than a game. I lost my cool.
I got angry, not for losing (I was used to that) but
because I wasn't proud about how I reacted.

Game 1: The first such game came when I was 8 or 9-years-old. It was well into November. Somehow, we had managed to advance to the finals in the county tournament. It poured on that gray autumn Saturday. As much as I liked playing in the rain, this was a touch too much. In fact, I think the referee brought a Sno-Cat with him in case the temperature dipped enough to change the rain to snow, and he'd have to rely on a more suitable way to patrol the field during play. After the game (which I think we lost, because man, that is the side to bet on), I got home and jumped into the shower to warm up my body. The hot water made my feet tingle so badly that if my parents asked, "Do you want to ride it out? or have them amputated?", I would have screamed: "Just get a f–king butter knife and let's do this for all I care!". Eventually, the temperature extremes evened out, but not before a fairly lengthy adjustment period. "There does not appear to be any permanent damage" are some of the happiest words in the English language. So that was the bad one.

Game 2: For some reason we played a team from another county, and man: they were large. There is no chance they were the same age as our squad. During halftime, we were handed orange slices and water. They received orange slices, water, and shaving cream with straight razors to trim their robust beards. By .542

seconds into the second half, my team was pretty
pissed off. Not because we were losing – the
sting of defeat had long since drifted well into
the recesses of our collective memories – but
because we were getting bounced around like pin
balls by these grown men who had clearly fought
in Vietnam. At some point, the ball magically
fell to my feet and some ogre bore down on me.
His beard and his mullet were waving in perfect
harmony as his wide strides rapidly closed the
gap between us. I am not a big guy, but I had a
fairly strong and very accurate kick, so I did
what I could: when the time was right, I rocketed
the ball straight into his hog.

I don't care what the difference is in size,
a well-struck (probably my best strike ever)
soccer ball to the hog is going to drop anyone.
And oh, did he ever drop. There was an audible
gasp from the sidelines as it became clear that his
familial line had just died. No one on the field
really knew what to do – it is not a foul to kick a
ball into someone's hog. Still, something needed
to be done. The referee blew his whistle and
gave a throw-in to the team that was now down a
player who was, in turn, down a hog. We were in
the middle of the field, and a throw-in made no
sense at all. But no one complained.

That was the angry game. I did not feel bad about trucking that dude's hog, I was just angry that I let that team get to me.

For the record:

Chrest, Brett; Midfield

Games Played: A lot

Goals Scored: 1 (At William S. James Elementary School against Hickory)

Hogs intentionally trucked: 1

Yoga

Yoga has turned into a very persistent fad. You might even be prone to removing the "fad" tag and upgrade the practice to "thing" or "international phenomenon". My wife has been doing yoga for several years – not quite before it took off, but not too far behind the curve either. Even before everyone had yoga pants, yoga mats, and drank yoga smoothies at yoga smoothie bars, she had a daily routine that would kill most humans. I know this. I tried it and it almost killed me. Luckily my "Willingness to Accept Defeat" gene is strong, and I tapped out before my heart, spleen or left lung exploded.

Seriously, if you are on one of those drugs that daytime TV ads warn you about re: impaired judgement, do not start yoga. If you

73

cannot be trusted to operate heavy machinery like a bulldozer, you cannot be trusted to make a good life decision regarding the structural integrity of your muscular system. You might not realize that every muscle is going to do its very best to forcibly eject itself through the pores in your skin.

Detective: "Have you determined the cause of death?"

Medical examiner: "I'm just now looking at the file and....what? They were on praxixlocrapazine and tried to do yoga. The cause of death for this man is – officially - 'being a moron'."

While it is true that I have a strong "Willingness to Accept Defeat" gene, it will not kick in until after my "Unable to Quit While I'm Behind" gene runs out of energy. So, if I get started, I tend to go all the way to the edge of the cliff.

Ask my wife about when we would play rummy together. Even the inanimate playing cards were telling me to quit after I lost 37 consecutive hands. So, I kept at it (yoga, not rummy). I learned that I had muscles I never knew about. I am over 40, and you can imagine how angry those muscles were when I finally started paying attention to them after years of neglect, including 15+ years of working at a desk.

My wife and I now do (most of, in my case) her routine daily. I do not fall down as much as I used to. I've even gotten to the point where I don't have to half-ass (most) poses, even those that once you have half-assed are really hard to convince yourself to full-ass. As the ancient Minoans once said: once half-assery is acceptable, full-assery is impossible.

Full disclosure: I have pieces of green duct tape on my yoga mat (yep – I have one) so I do not cheat in regard to foot placement.

A few weeks in and I feel good. I am stronger and more limber (something I NEVER thought I would say). I am still working on the restorative/meditation part. These are elements that are tough to conquer when I am trying to remember which leg to lift and there are two kids in the other room throwing live hand grenades at each other (at least that's what it sounds like). I know that this will fade for me. I will get tired of it. The kids are older and more able to get heavier/tougher to reach stuff for me. I no longer need to be quite as strong and/or limber.

In the time after I retire, I will at least know enough about yoga to properly revel in my wife's accomplishments. She can already tackle all the key elements that are part of yoga-ing:

Physical Health: "I can still kick your ass. Watch how long I can hold this pose, even with more than 80% of my blood rapidly pooling in my cranium."

Emotional Health: "I'm still at peace even though someone just spilled a gallon of orange juice onto the kitchen floor."

Dealing With Dopes Like Me: "We always start with the right leg – why is this such a recurring issue for you? What kind of barbarian starts anything with the left?"

One aspect of yoga I will not miss is the larger yoga community. Like all esoteric communities, the yoga community can get quite jerkish. This is especially so when they branch out and into the world, like via YouTube. I will not miss that part, and it is not a feature of my wife's practice.

"You know how I know you don't have a job, YouTuber? You can do the Crumpled Lotus, which means that you have been practicing for 80 hours a week for 8 years. Let's just go back to that dog face pose."

The mental side of yoga was fun to get acquainted with – the idea of physical exertion leading to mental/emotional restoration. If I am lucky, I will find a way to convert the physical side of watching baseball on TV into mental health.

And, if nothing else, yoga has reaffirmed my belief in gravity. Trust me: it is still present in this world and disproportionately affects people starting to try yoga.

Running

I have thin legs. The kind of thin legs that make ostriches bury their heads in the sand so they can talk about me without me knowing about it.

My legs are so thin that, many times, when my wife and I eat out, a lecherous glutton with roughly 4.6 ounces of prime rib stuck between his/her teeth would ask to borrow one of my legs to use as a toothpick.

I oblige, of course. Lending a leg to assist with dental health is a very neighborly thing to do. That is how we roll in Maryland. Just return the favor and return my leg in its original condition. I do not need the wad of medium done meat.

Multiple popsicle manufacturers have requested access to my legs to allow their research and development departments to design more efficient means to ram wood into frozen sucrose. If you have had a popsicle in the last 20 years, there is a good chance that my right leg was the template for the stick design.

My wife's legs are thicker than mine – I happen to know this because I spend a fair amount of time with her. Back when school was in session, she'd pick the kids up from school and walk them home with some of our neighbors. If I was lucky, when I was still working in an office, I could get out of work early. I would drive down our road as they were all still walking home, look off to the side, and wave at the crew as I passed.

This was especially fulfilling if it was cold and/or raining.

I was in a dry, climate-controlled car. And they were not. At the time, I drove a car with heated seats. Any time this situation arose, I turned them on, even if my buns were already nicely toasted.

Trudy McTreetrunks

One afternoon, my wife and Trudy were walking together (with the kids), profiled. I could see both sets of legs as I looked at the kids frolicking down the sidewalk. Let us be clear – this was not to leer at anyone, it is just that kids

tend to be smaller than adults, and my eye
direction was along that plane.

Trudy McTreetrunks is – obviously – a
pseudonym. Do not bother Googling her. But, if
you cannot resist and find something funny, let
me know.

My legs are puny compared to my wife's,
but at that moment I could see (they were both
wearing yoga pants. I live in suburban Maryland
– it is a thing) that my wife's legs were puny
compared to Trudy's. Seriously, instead of
taking a kid to/from school, she could carry 3-4
mid-sized Kias. Or a battleship. Or some
combination thereof.

Shamed that I could not haul a large
naval vessel four nautical miles, I decided to stop
skipping "leg day" when working out. I even
started to run places. Surely, self-propulsion
would beef things up.

Full disclosure: I skip lots of days. Arm
day, chest day, neck day, and even glute day.

So, per my usual implementation of a
plan, I over-did the leg stuff, and my legs
became rather sore. Not just the usual suspects,
either. Even my toes got in on the "Party of
Woe".

My entire lower body was "sore AF" as the kids would say.

When it became a physical burden, due to excessive legwork, to perform basic activities such as "walking from the bedroom to the kitchen," I asked myself a question:

What am I doing?

A fraction of a fraction of a fraction of the world's population will ever see my legs. My wife, who is the only person I care about regarding my physical appearance, seems reasonably OK with the situation. She has not left me for an Italian race car driver (yet).

"Mid-life crisis" is something that crossed my mind as I struggled to saunter down the stairs...but that is not it. I did not move to Guyana to teach kids how to mess with squirrels. I did not even purchase new exercise equipment that would be – and I know this is a hack joke – something to hang laundry on in 2.65 weeks.

It was, in my estimation, a "mid-life impulse". Nothing more than a perceived deficiency that – while meaningless – I felt that I needed to rectify. I have felt that in the past, and my position now is to recognize it and deal with it in a practical manner that is not very likely to kill me.

Starting to run again in the throes of summer in Maryland is rough, weather-wise. The humidity here is epic, and even doing a push-up can cause someone without sweat glands to sweat. You can imagine what running two miles with glands can do. It leads to dehydration which then requires rehydration which leads to having to pee more. That requires a trip from the bedroom to the bathroom on sore legs and, well, you get the idea. It is quite the domino effect.

Still, here I am though, getting back into the running game (which is less fun than a game of Risk).

Is this folly? Probably. I am no stranger to follies.

An example of a past folly?

Years ago, I decided that I wanted to learn Spanish, and you know where it got me?

"No me gusta la langosta."

That is not even true: I love lobster.

Triathlon

One of my many talents that border on "smarmy" is the ability to cleverly oversell my athletic excellence. For example, some time ago my wife decided that she wanted to do a triathlon. Triathlons are a combination of something I hate doing (running), something I don't really mind (biking), and something that confuses me (swimming). Pools are for floating and getting Vitamin D. Not propelling oneself from one wall to the other and then repeating the process for dozens of laps. Still, it all kind of balanced out. So, since there are still a few fibers in my body that are misguidedly competitive, I agreed to join her on this adventure of physical agony.

"Let's do this together sweetheart!"

Plus, I could use it to get out of going to happy hours with co-workers I really did not like.

"Sorry Bill, I'm training tonight. Maybe next...<trails off>..."

Thus, I would find myself trying to keep up with my wife at various outdoor venues near our house. We ran through the trails of Central Maryland. Biked for unnecessarily long distances on roads/trails that seemed engineered to include more hills than necessary. As with any good hill however, if you get up it, you have the chance to go down it. Progress without exertion is right up my alley.

We even swam hundreds of laps in a pool filled with water that the county must have been intentionally cooling through some insidious machine.

One night, a polar bear was complaining to the pool manager that the water was too warm. The manager, whose sense of self-preservation kicked in when a potentially violent mammal confronted him, disappeared into some shack on site. Within minutes, the water was so cold that I lost two toes. They grew back.

The other odd thing about the pool was that it was obnoxiously small. One full lap is something like ten meters, which means that to knock out a cool 1000M requires a staggering 100 laps. I can barely count to 100 when my lungs are not on fire.

Still, onward we went, inching ever closer to attaining a level of fitness that would make doing this %$#@ing thing slightly less lethal. We were so dedicated that, during a vacation to Ireland a few weeks before the event, we went for a run through the Irish countryside. It was beautiful…I am told. Due to the hilliness of the area, my primary focus was less on the scenery than it was on ensuring that my lungs would not forcibly eject themselves from my chest cavity.

Shout out to Ireland, by the way. Thanks to the internet's merciless insistence on collecting stats, I can see that my website gets a small but steady number of hits that trace back to the Emerald Isle.

If you are reading, and not just bots, I enjoyed Kilkenny more than Dublin. Not ragging on Dublin, I just thought Kilkenny was a delightful place.

When we returned from our trip abroad, we finished our carefully choreographed training regimen, including a dry run that did not kill us. We were as ready as we would ever be. And by that, I mean we were as ready as our schedules allowed. We could – especially me – have been more ready.

It is Race Day!

We woke up early on the "Day of Doom" and drove about an hour to the race site. We had spent the previous night at my parents' house, on a pull-out sofa bed – exactly the way the pros draw it up for peak performance. Upon arrival, we parked, off-loaded the bikes, and queued up to begin the North East Triathlon, held in the northeastern town of North East, MD, along the – you guessed it – North East River. Cecil County is not known for their intellectual rigor vis-a-vis naming things. It was thrilling. I swam! I biked! I ran (most of the time)! I finished! The swimming went well enough. I am a rather good swimmer, even in open water, and while I was not winning anything, I was on the happy side of mediocrity and finished ahead of lots of people.

My rousing success in the water quickly took a dark turn. I am not a strong cyclist in the best of times, and this time I was riding on paved streets on a mountain bike with nubby tires. The equipment issue slowed me down that much more, and within a few miles people were regularly whizzing past me with such frequency that I swore they were all lapping me – there could not be that many people!

All that was left was a run. I managed that fairly well, even though I did take a pause near the end. My in-laws had set up right before the finishing 100 meters. I stopped and asked that they take my picture because "you ain't going to ever see this again." A quick shot or two and I was off to cross the finish line.

There is actually a funny story about the finish. When we got married, my wife's wedding day gift to me was two basketball jerseys to symbolize that we were on the same team. It is a quaint thought, but she put "Chrest" across the front of the jersey, not the back like – literally – every other name-bearing jersey in existence.

Days before the race, she suggested that we should wear the jerseys for the race. I agreed, even knowing that I would look like a rube with my last name on my chest, because it was a very nice thought (I mean that sincerely.)

Guess who forgot to pack her jersey. Not me. There was one rube in that race, and he is typing these words.

So, it came to pass that, during the final sprint (read: walk) to the finish line, a carnival barker would spot your bib number, check the roster of competitors to match number to name, and say something like: "Congratulations Chester McStrongabs!"

For me it was: "Great finish Br...oh, he has his name on the front of his shirt."

Here is the Kicker

While it is, in fact, true that we completed the North East Triathlon, there is a bit of an asterisk. We did the weenie version. The sprint tri – roughly half the distances in all three events than the real version. But you know what? We all got the same commemorative t-shirts. The ones that made no distinction between real athletes who did the whole course and athletes like me. I wore that shirt threadbare with the idea that strangers would look at me and think: "that guy's a triathlete!" Maybe they even told their kids, over family dinner, that they saw a triathlete on their way home from work.

The word "hornswoggling" appears prominently on my resume.

Hot Tubs

That brings us to last night. My wife and I decided to have a nice soak in the old' hot tub. When we do so, I will go out first and sit for a few minutes to think and reflect. Then, she will come out and we will talk about whatever. After that, I will go into the house a few minutes early so she can sit, think, and reflect. When I went out last night, the tub was quiet – not cycling or anything. As I got in, with the water still, I realized that a still hot tub is nothing more than a heated outdoor pool.

I swam around 50 laps in the pool last night. What did your lazy asses do?

The "Currently Reading" Fad

"The reading of all good books is like a conversation with the finest minds of past centuries." - Rene Descartes

Where I work, it is fashionable to add a "currently reading" list of 2–3 books to a user's signature block. It is a clever idea, and I enjoy getting — at times — to learn a little bit about my colleagues' interests. I say "at times" because some lists are way too telling. If you are currently reading *"How to Evade Capture by Colombian Drug Cartels"*, *"Is that Wound Infected? Find Out in Three Easy Steps!"*, and *"Rain Forest Remedies for Large-Caliber Gunshot Wounds"* you have made— or will soon make — a series of very poor life decisions.

Conversely, you can also get people with exceptionally bland lists which reveal nothing about the sender. *"Car"*, *"Re-usable Grocery Bag"*, and *"4.5 Pounds of Head Cheese"*? Really? Are those books? Or did you just get back from the supermarket?

I could also go for some sort of icon that indicates that a neutral third-party has verified the "currently reading" list. I find it hard to believe that this is a real list for someone:

- *"Origins of the Bangladesh Army: 1634–2009"* by Sabir Abdus Samee
- *"Handbook of Borehole Acoustics and Rock Physics for Reservoir Characterization"* by Vimal Saxena

- *"Cyanobacteria Biotechnology"* by Rev. Nerd Nerdington

So far, I have managed to stave off the desire to add a list that includes *"Dash's Belly Ache: A Book for Children Who Can't or Won't Poop"* by Wendy Hayden. (It is part of the *"Dash Learns Life Skills Series"*. I can only imagine what else is on there, but I hope that *"Dash's Big Meal: Dash Learns Modern Cannibal Recipes: Forward by Paula Dean"* makes the cut.) So…

Currently reading

So here is my list. However, in order to dodge some of the pitfalls I laid out above, I'll first introduce the book, possibly liberally cutting-and-pasting from Wikipedia. Then, I'll give two reasons as to why I am reading that particular book. One is satirical and/or humorous. The other is for real. Try to guess which is which!

My wife, e'er the killjoy, thinks that this is a fool's errand — just a snapshot in time. But…at least two of these books should have lasting impacts on me. It remains to be seen if the third, a murder mystery about an immigrant who was mutilated after being killed, will have a similar effect. Also, these books are long. This post will be just as relevant when I turn 50 in a few years.

With that said, here my list:

- *"When the Light of the World was Subdued, Our Songs Came Through: a Norton Anthology of Native Nations Poetry"* edited by Joy Harjo
- *"The Spirit of Laws"* by Charles-Louis de Secondat baron de Montesquieu
- *"The Alienist"* by Caleb Carr

I can honestly say that I am currently reading all three.

"When the Light of the World was Subdued, Our Songs Came Through: a Norton Anthology of Native Nations Poetry" edited by Joy Harjo

No real mystery here. This is a collection of poems — an "anthology", if you will — of Native poetry. It was edited by, you guessed it, Joy Harjo. The breadth of the collection is impressive. This big old book covers centuries of poetry over various geographic regions (one of the regions is NOT titled *"That Place that Refers to 'Soda' as 'Pop'"*). I just started out — it seemed like a solid pick-up right before spending a few days reading, writing, and avoiding rattlesnakes with the family at a secluded mountain cabin in West Virginia. So far, so good. I won't quote any poems here out of concern for copyright issues. (That's not a joke

— I honestly don't know if there are any law-talking' hiccups.)

Why this book (first version)

Native Americans are cool! Tonto was a Native American, and he was pretty cool. He'd pal around and help the Lone Ranger do lone ranger-ish things. Like, put on his mask and Velcro his boots. (I guess that makes him less of a "lone" ranger and more of a "friends with benefits" ranger, but I digress.) Tonto and the Lone Ranger must have done good things, like help Frodo blow up the Death Star, because Loney wore a white hat.

A plucky group of Native Americans — including the last member of the Mohican tribe — even managed to spice up a James Fenimore Cooper novel. In the middle of a 15-page run-on sentence about changing a door handle on the Kentucky frontier in 1743, one of them up and killed a French soldier in a delightfully gory manner.

But wait, there is more! Pocahontas seduced a white guy. Geronimo was such a daring bad ass that an entire generation of youth would yell his name before trying to jump over a large canyon on a bike with a rusty chain.

All of these examples are 100000000000% true and not at all stereotypical.

I want to learn more. Especially how Tonto helped Frodo with that whole Death Star thing. Didn't they already blow that up at the end of Episode 4?

Why this book (second version)

Native poetry is cool — much cooler than some hack Disney mash up where Sitting Bull helps the USS Enterprise broker a peace deal between Romulus and Krypton. Think about this *real-life* mash up:

One of the poets is a native member of the Cherokee tribe who fought for the South during the Civil War. Shortly before he was killed in battle, he wrote the poem in question to a woman back home. She would later marry the soldier's older brother. Some of the poems in this anthology inspired my children to write poetry.

I tried to think of additional reasons for why I wanted to read this, but I really can't: that's just one example of an exceptional and real story contained herein, and the effect it can have on the reader.

"The Spirit of Laws" by Charles-Louis de Secondat Baron de Montesquieu

The Baron is one of the great thinkers of the Enlightenment. Along with such notables as

Immanuel U-Kant-Touch-This, John It's-a-Locke, and Michael Jurassic-Park-Made-More-$$$-Than-All-Y'all-Crichton, their works form the backbone of modern Western political thought. In this whopper of a tome, Montesquieu starts off with the laws of nature and paddles upstream for two volumes until he proves, beyond a shadow of a doubt, that the In-and-Out double-double is tragically overrated.

Why this book (first version)

I like laws. Spirits seem pretty cool as well. I just wish that spirits would talk to me about laws. My legal seances are awfully dry — I'm the only one who talks about tort reform when the candles are lit. It seems to me that a book all about the Spirit of Laws would be helpful in opening up the proverbial floor for debate. The damn thing is 700 pages stretched over two volumes. "How to" books/articles should only exceed six pages if they involve some sort of nuclear fusion. I'm a good chunk into this train wreck and I am still no closer to mystically conversing with Themis, Daniel Webster, or even a dead NFL referee.

Here's a tip for the sake of brevity: don't talk to me about what I already know. So far, Chuck the Boring de Whocaresquieu has spent a ton of time on defining laws and the types of government. As a father, I adhere to one type of

94

government — dadpotism — and know all I need to know about laws. Laws are nothing more than if/then constructs that are hopefully punitive enough to prevent my kids from doing something I don't want them to do. "If you reinsulate the attic, clean out all of the air ducts, and plunge the toilet that has been overflowing for the last three days, THEN you can read another graphic novel.

(Next on Oldest's list? "Wolverine's Bottom Itching: A Book for Comic Book Heroes Who Can't or Won't Clean Up Properly", part of the X-Men Learn Life Skills Series. Admittedly, I kind of get the appeal. On one hand, Wolverine heals quickly. On the other hand, that's still an awful lot of blood to temporarily fix a problem that could be conquered by better wiping habits.)

Nonetheless, I hope to get through this section and be chatting up dead litigators by Volume II of the book.

Why this book (second version)

I actually enjoy reading dense philosophy. In college, I came within four ounces of caring enough about it to tack on a philosophy minor. However, I decided to get a job and earn money rather than pay money to argue with someone over whether or not my recollection of the taste of an overripe peach was an impression or a memory and whether or not I had *a piori* knowledge of stone fruit. I've read this work— and many others like it — before. The joy of comprehensive tomes is the ability to read and reread with certain other angles in mind. This time 'round, as a newly minted educator, I'm more focused on social/societal impacts and governmental responsibilities.

If nothing else, I'd like to head into the academic year with a heaping helping of logical thought on my noodle. I've only scratched the surface on educational perennialism (the idea that certain key skills should be taught year after year), but parts of it seem appealing (I reserve the right to change my mind). I figure that the ability to read, digest, and critically think about complex issues is one of those skills that won't get stale (like my humor).

"The Alienist" by Caleb Carr

This novel is a crime drama set in 1899, New York. Its main characters are a drunk, a quack, a dead immigrant and – oops sorry for some reason — Teddy Roosevelt. It is the first in a series, but — so far — it seems like a good series. One that you can really get into for a period of time (like Dash Learns Life Skills) and not one of those never-ending drivel-fests that feature Elvish case law studies (like the Lord of the Rings). I'm also a fan of historical fiction, and this fits the bill.

Why this book (first version)

This book came out in 1994, but I only recently learned that it is now a TV show. If a TV executive thinks it is good enough to regurgitate the original content with superfluous "updates", well...that is good enough for me! I figure that binge-watching the series will be a fitting reward for trudging through actual literature. Do you remember when Michael Bay rebooted "Hamlet" to change a scene to have a cyber-Hamlet blast a half-alien Polonius — who was hidden behind a cloaking device — in "Hamlet: The Danish Ghost Wars"? It was perfection!

The book also purports to be about police reform, led by Teddy Roosevelt. That Teddy Roosevelt. He of "walk like a boss and carry a high caliber handgun" fame. During those sections of the book, the body count would certainly rise like my cholesterol (the bad kind) after four hours in a Golden Corral.

Why this book (second version)

As I sit here reading and writing on the side of a mountain top, molested only by the sounds of frolicking deer who are smart enough to stay on the happy side of the "no hunting" signs, I am also facing down a trip to New York City in a few weeks. I've been there plenty of times before for work (although this time is for a family trip) and know enough to know that it is a big city.

I like small cities. Baltimore is more my style. It is a few square blocks of well-policed tourist areas, chain restaurants, and two publicly funded professional-level sports stadiums. Marylanders do not know the math that funds such athletic endeavors that lurk behind state lotteries. I have read that there are other parts of the city that are less well-to-do. Those parts of Baltimore do not have moderately interesting architecture, large fish tanks, or Mr. Trash Wheel. Therefore, I have no interest.

(Mr. Trash Wheel is a moored vessel that removes trash from the mouth of the Jones Falls River as it enters Baltimore's Inner Harbor. Rubbish from the streets of Baltimore is flushed into storm drains that empty into the Jones Falls River.)

Nonetheless, what better way to get in a New York state of mind than to read about real people (Jacob Riis, T-Rizzle, etc.) and the hunt for a vicious serial killer in the turn-of-the-century Big Apple?

There you have it: what I am currently reading

For the near future, during my downtime, I will be alternating between poetry, philosophy, and a race to catch a killer who doesn't like young, male prostitutes. I'd love to hear about your own list, but here's a tip: Make sure that any recommendation 1) doesn't suck and 2) is about what it says it is about.

If your book is "How to Conquer Rome", I damn well better be prepared to lead an army down the Via del Corso by the end. I am not looking for some tired allegory about getting over major life hurdles like eating right or exercising. There are seven hills of Rome (Quirinal, Esquiline, Capitoline, etc.). I am looking for a read out on the strategic value of each. I have no interest in any information on the nutritional values of the seven hills of fried chicken (Cajun, Korean, Hawaiian, Kentucky, etc.).

Even a poorly conceived – but well-intended – reading list is better than nothing at all.

Telling a Tall Tale to Help Out a Friend

"Not as hot as the summer of '88 when the chickens laid fried eggs and the babies cried sawdust." - Pecos Bill

The set up

My wife's friend is fixing to hike the famed El Camino trail in Spain this fall and is keen to write all about it when she gets back. The friend was a little apprehensive about doing a good job of capturing the pilgrimage. My wife is the better writer but can be less-than-adventurous. I'm not too terrible at writing, but I have a pretty vivid imagination. So, I offered to write a fictional account of my trip to Spain. The friend is free to cut/paste/alter anything I've written here to help her out.

In all seriousness, I love independent travel. I like hiking and being in nature. My wife, who is really into the three Ms of healthy living - Mindfulness, Meditation, MiraLAX - taught me this:

"Mindfulness is not a mechanical process. It is developing a very gentle, kind, and creative awareness to the present moment."

- Amit Ray

But seriousness is not why you are here. You are here to learn about how I discovered that the German word for diarrhea is - hilariously - durchfall. So, we begin...

Prelude to a dream

My Christmas Card. Public domain image as altered by author.

It all started last Christmas. About a decade ago, my cousin won several lottery jackpots using the numbers 3-2-7-8 (the alpha-

numeric code for FART). Instead of doing
something cool with the winnings, like buying a
NASCAR team, he decided to start a
philanthropic enterprise. Every December 25, we
would all be "treated" to a lengthy slideshow
about something stupid. Two years ago, he
allegedly learned from an Amazonian tribe how
to make a 5G cell phone using just some acai
berries, monkey fur, and a few sloth's teeth.
Enough was enough. I sent out the above image
as my holiday card with the promise of a show
that would be - wait for it - OUT OF THIS
WORLD!

It did not go well. Apparently, Elon
Musk has not been to space. That is not what his
arm looks like. Uranus is way too large in the
picture. Disgraced, I vowed to take what was left
from the money my cousin had given all of us to
come up with a trip that was exotic and fake-
able. That is, I needed enough "evidence" to
"prove" that I had done what I claimed.

Settling on hiking in Spain

A semi-exotic hike seemed like the most
obvious choice. I would not have to do anything
amazing like cure a disease. It seemed relatively
safe, as long as I did not go to the Himalayas or
Chicago. There were all kinds of neat countries
that, per their Wikipedia page, did not suck too
badly. Some even had relatively low occurrences

of natural disasters like tornadoes, micro-black holes, and underwhelming national parks. After a few blackberry and chili pepper Ka'chava smoothies that I had spiked with Kahlua, it came to me in a dream: Spain, aka España, aka the Land of the Tapas. It was time to gear up and get planning (Step 1: obtain my own Amazon Prime account).

The most famous trail in Spain is El Camino, a network of routes that all seem to end up in Galicia. Perfect. A foreign country AND a trek with a purpose: tracing the steps of a dead guy. To make sure that this would be just exotic enough, I started dropping trail-related lingo into everyday conversations to see if friends or family knew what I was talking about.

Me: "O's bullpen really crapped the bed again last night. Webber pitches like he is from Santiago de Compostela, amiright?"

Uncle Tommy: "Wha....you are into compost heaps now?"

Me <to self>: "Swish."

I decided to take the Camino Del Norte route. This version of the famous trek runs a whopping 513 miles. Here is the thing, however: all I need to do is SAY I walked the whole thing and have a fitness tracker on a device that actually went 513 miles. If you think I am above paying someone to walk my phone across a foreign country just so I can say that I did it, you clearly do not know me. To bolster my claim, my new Amazon Prime account shows that I spent a lot of money on hiking stuff - like the Emergency Zone Eco Gel Sanitation Set with Privacy Shelter, Hygienic Waste Disposal System for Camping, Hiking, Emergency Preparedness. My Travelocity profile shows that I bought the relevant airfare.

From a digital footprint point of view, I went to Spain with hiking gear and moved 513 miles from the starting point to the end destination. How much ground did I actually cover? That is a secret I will take to my grave. Or a Hollywood producer interested in buying my story.

The first mile

This was, by far, the most exciting moment. I rose early - the sun was still tucked behind the magnificent Pyrenees Mountains. The ambient light from Earth's star was just strong enough to cast a shadow westward, pointing me in the direction of my travels. It was Saturday, April 1. Luckily, my phone had plenty of battery power and a strong enough signal to take advantage of the new grocery store deals of the week. 15% off of 15 pounds of Ka'chava? Yes sir! I will have quite the feast when I return home.

I crossed myself, took a deep breath, drank a can of sangria, and put my right foot forward. I was off. The earth (and the empty can of sangria) crunched under my weight. In no time at all, I would be basking in the warm glow of St. James in Santiago de Compostela! My head was swimming with feelings of awe, fear, wonder, and a dull pain from that sangria that was - inexplicably - not vegan. A few feet from the first mile marker, I decided to take a leak so as to cross that Rubicon as pure and waste-free as possible. This was, after all, a spiritual sojourn.

I took off my pack and fetched my hiking potty. After 15 minutes, I had set up the privacy shelter. It took another 20 to work up the courage to go, and a solid 30 minutes more to re-pack everything. I figured that less than 90 minutes was a good time for the endeavor. With an empty bladder jangling inside of my abdominal cavity, I snapped a few selfies and went on my way.

By the time I had finished updating my social media accounts, and texted my friends/family, it was time to hunker down for the night. I had done it: like so few before me, I survived Day 1 on the trail.

Life on the Trail

Within a few days, I had really hit my stride and had a pretty set daily routine. At 8AM, my white noise maker would switch over and start playing K-pop songs to gently wake me. I'd set up, use, and dismantle the outdoor potty. This would take 1 – 2 hours depending on if I had to take a dump or not. Next up was my daily tweet.

Great day on the trail yest. Covered lots of ground! #fitness4life #spiritual #kachava #kachavalifestyle #kachavafamily #cleanse

Breakfast was usually No Bake Maple Tahini Ka'chava protein bars or a Ka'chava Superfood Smoothie bowl. It took an hour or two to knock out a few miles, at which point I would stop for a sugar-free Mountain Dew and Ka'chava Superfood Snack Mix. I frequently skipped lunch. This was mostly to keep up with my intermittent fasting, but, if I am being honest, all of my superfoods made my stomach super unhappy when I tried to ram un-super solids down into it.

No worries though – the afternoon was the best time to be alert. During my pre-hike research Google told me that this was the best time to see Spain's wildlife. Per the Goog, the Iberian lynx, Iberian brown bear, and several Iberian mollusks are most active between 2 –

4PM Standard Eurotime. I have no idea where "Iberia" is, but it must really suck since all its animals left and came to Spain. Sadly, my Apple Animal I-tracker stayed eerily silent. (I did "see" a ton of Pokémon though. If Pokémon Go was still a thing, I would be a PokéBoss.) The flora was no better. Spanish olives are bitter little wankers with something hard in the middle. Plus, there were not any with little red squiggles of plant matter jammed inside. American olives pwn their Spanish cousins.

Afternoon was also the best time to meet people.

The people of the trail

Bound by our common goal of finally being able to one up cousin Marty McTravelguy at family holiday gatherings, we became a close-knit group. Apparently, overachieving family members are kind of like Santa Claus: each culture has its own variation on the theme. I became quite popular amongst some of the more common countries, even earning several nicknames. The Germans called me Herr Durchfall, possibly due to the deep brown color and semi-liquid consistency of my Ka'chava. I was el Tortuga Electrico thanks to the solar powered battery charger that I used for my Apple family of devices and my...deliberate...pace. The unimaginative English simply called me "the

Bloke with a Loo on 'is Back". In fairness, I was toting a dump station on my back.

To add to the camaraderie, I would cheerfully reply with a culturally sensitive quip in their native tongues: "Ich bin ein Berliner!" "No me gusta la langosta!" "So you cook it all in a sheep's uterus?" And so on.

A subset of the traveling menagerie - a group that seemed more motivated to make it to the end - claimed to be heading across Spain to see the remains of St. James the Greater. I guess if you are going to eschew modern transportation methods (y'all ever hear of a Tesla?) to trek through a land of crappy olive trees and invisible animals, best to do it to see a greater saint and not some D-minus religious guy.

A snake in the grass/the end of the road

At about the same time I started to notice that I was running low on my prescription Super Sack Support Briefs with AirTech Ventilation Technology, a lot of my travel partners began to hike with an extra pep in their steps. This kind of drastic improvement was not natural and could only be caused by custom made undies. I confirmed with my support team, and they too had noticed a sharp decline in undie inventory.

My support team was truly heroic. They laid off, just beyond visual range, and were ready to resupply me at a moment's notice. They also crucially brought me the L'il Trailmaster Ninja Foodie Blender I relied on for my smoothies.

A quick check of my iSupersack app confirmed that the closest outlet was in Toulouse, France, making such a speedy delivery all but impossible. Only one conclusion could be reached: my travel friends - the very ones who gave me endearing nicknames like Mr. Diarrhea - had betrayed my confidence and were ganking my drawers. I couldn't continue on with these (very comfortable) Janus-faced asps. I called my expedition director, Jens, and we agreed to move to the final step of Operation *Falsis Principiis*. Immediately, a pre-determined lineup of couriers began shuttling my phone to the end of the trail, under strict orders to continue at my previously established pace.

I hopped a Gulf Stream, and awaited my phone's arrival, at a 4-star hotel in style with shrimp cocktails and all the sangria I could drink.

El fin de hiking in Spain

Days later, while sitting on my balcony overlooking Galicia's center, I was thumbing through all of the "selfies" that my team took on my behalf. It was all, on aggregate, worth it. Just take a look at my 2021 Xmas card:

My new Christmas Card. Public domain image as altered by author.

Oh, That Game with the Small Holes and Tinier Balls

"Be content with what you have;
rejoice in the way things are.
When you realize there is nothing lacking,
the whole world belongs to you." - Lao
Tzu

What homage to the middle years of the human life cycle is complete without a little golf? Only here is the thing: I only really golfed when I was in my early twenties – I have since given up the sport for all intents and purposes, though I do not rule out a return to the links in the future. In my early 20s, I was in between stints at a 4-year university and found myself working overnight at a major retailer. A team of 8-10 of us had the store to ourselves as we unloaded the truck and stocked the shelves, astonished over how much deodorant that store went through. (As the ones stocking on a daily basis, we knew how much of what – generally — was sold that day.) Even with a fair amount of jack-assery and an appetite for practical jokes, we took pride in getting the job done and not leaving anything left for the dayside crew.

In between tasks we would take time to race the motorized shopping carts and hide 12-packs of soda in the baler (when the first person on the day shift used the baler to crunch down a bunch of cardboard, it would make a disturbing noise as the volume of the cans rapidly decreased and the mass started to ooze Dr. Pepper).

In short, it was the best job of my life. At the end of most shifts in the spring and summer, we would grab breakfast and head to a local public course to tee it up at 7:30AM on a weekday. We always had enough for a foursome, and many times a full enough roster for two foursomes.

Hal

Most of the time, we had the course to ourselves and a regular named Hal. Hal was in his 80's and there every day with his old-school handcart for his golf bag. The bag was well into its second 50 years of service and the only clubs that were younger were replacements for those that Hal had broken over the years.

Since the course switched back and forth so much, we would usually see Hal when he was playing the 5th and we were on the 2nd.

"Hal, how's she playing today?"

"Like shit. Hope you boys have better luck."

Every day.

By the time we finished, Hal was in the clubhouse, and we would buy him lunch and a drink. Tuna salad with two dill pickle spears, Ruffles original flavor chips and a vodka tonic.

One afternoon, as Hal was hobbling to his car, Kevin finally asked Hal why he did not use a golf cart. Clearly, at least part of his impairment came from walking 18-holes 5-times a week (the rest we chalked up to the vodka tonic). Jangling the keys his right hand in to an old Honda Civic that was probably older than we were, Hal opened the driver's side door and replied:

"Can't drive."

Sometimes, we had to mingle with "real" golfers

Other times, if there were six of us playing, two of us would get partnered up with a random pair. I think it was the starter just messing with us – we knew everyone who worked at the course, and we gave as good as we got in terms of jokes. I distinctly recall one time when my buddy Pete and I got paired with the very personifications of golf wannabes. Clad head to toe with all the very finest in golf attire, they wielded clubs that cost more than my car, and golf balls designed to auto-seek the hole. In short, they were very formidable duffers.

Not that we cared about losing – Hal, who could not drive the car he drove to/from the golf course – routinely shot better than all of us – we just wanted to have an enjoyable time. And everyone on that course knew that these pricks were going to do all that they could (admittedly unintentionally) to ruin that simple ambition. Think of it this way: they brought $1,000+ of equipment to a public course that had grass on about 12 of the 18 greens, or 66%. With so few actual greens, it was impossible to get a good "greens in regulation" ratio.

"It only took three shots to hit the dirt patch surrounding the hole...does that count? And what are the rules for hitting a water hazard on the green?"

It did not take long for team "White Golf Pants" to confirm the worst: not only did they look the part of a killjoy, but they also used (misused?) all the golf lingo of a killjoy. I was up first to get the round started – a dogleg to the right that played ~400yds – and promptly clubbed a sharply hit ground ball around 100 yards into right field. Short, but right on the edge of the fairway.

"Oh! A worm burner, eh? Try a more elevated club," said the one called Brian, late–50s and retired – allegedly – with a yacht and a condominium on Top Sail Island. The other tool was up next – I forget his name – and laced a high arcing shot that hooked way left. Nonetheless, cue Brian: "That'll find fairway!"

Other guy: "Boooooo-yaaaah!"

Yes, it found a fairway. The 16th fairway and Other Guy had "advanced" the ball...100 yards. Instead of 300 yards to the pin (like me), this chucklehead was fist bumping his buddy over being 500 yards away.

On it went. By the 9th hole, Pete actually aimed his tee shot at our golf cart hoping that the ball would ricochet and hit one of our playing partners. It was a stunningly bold play, since we weren't exactly known for our accuracy. The plan did not work as desired. The ball just shot off into the woods, but I think Dumb and Dumberer got the point because they did not have anything "clever" to add. They did, however, continue to congratulate themselves on shots that were mediocre at best.

"That'll play!" It is in a tree.

"No worries with that one!" Except for the "worry" that the ball is under 4-feet of water. Luckily for them, they were the only people ever to play that course with a name brand ball, so finding it in the muck among all the "Nyke" brand balls wasn't tough.

The 13th hole was downhill, the "green" about 20 feet lower than the tee box. In plain view of one of the groundskeepers, I did a golf cart e-brake stop en route to my tee shot. The balding tires on that cart carved a 10-yard swath of doom into the fairway. The groundskeeper, Ed, just looked as if to say, "point taken".

By the end of the round, after we had customarily blasted a Happy Gilmore-ish tee shot off of the 18th tee, we retreated to the clubhouse to meet up with everyone else. They had finished 30+ minutes ahead of us – both of the special breed of chuckleheads that we played with would insist on finding all of their wayward $50/piece balls. Pete and I, meanwhile, were OK giving a cursory 1-minute look in the general direction of where we had whacked a 25-cent X-out ball before giving up and invoking the "Play it from wherever you want rule".

The 19th hole

Everyone was there, laughing hysterically – as they should have – at our misfortune. Hal even bought us each a Coors Light. He looked us dead in the eye and said something like: "If you boys can't drive and need a ride home, I can take you back", while sucking down the end of what was not his first vodka tonic of the day.

(Just to close the book on that episode, Brian and "Other Guy" complained about Pete and me to the manager. We were not as friendly as we could have been, in their estimation. Everyone had a good laugh, especially when Pete noted that his shot missed the mark when he was trying to brain Brian off the tee.)

The end of the road

But, back to the course the next day – it was almost certainly a better experience (I never recall going to the "old tool shed" for playing partners two days in a row). The good days were exactly what we wanted/needed out of golf. Real golf was not for us. I know a lot of people who love the game/sport/activity and spend what it takes to be reasonably good. But I do not have time, money, or desire to (re) assemble my golf game. I also don't have an overnight retail job that allows me to golf with my buddies (and Hal!) long before normal humans get to the course.

By the time we were moving on from this chapter of our lives, my decline was already starting to show. I hit the beverage cart with a ball – 90% of which's cooler ice was melted by 8:00AM – twice (unintentionally). Another friend mishit a ball onto a road that ran adjacent to the course and did not even bother to try and scamper out, into traffic, to hit his next shot. Clearly, we were a band whose time had come and gone.

The only thing left for us in golf was to join the local farm fair circuit with one hit wonders and over-the-hillers.

"Coming up next, right after the tractor pull and the hog racin': Blue Oyster Cult will play 'Don't Fear the Reaper'. Then, Bachman Turner

119

*Overdrive will play 'Taking Care of Business'.
In between, the Sad Hacks from Harford County
will recreate some of their most hilarious golf
shots."*

Either that, or we could go back to real
life and try to make something of ourselves.
Spoiler alert: I have not been to a farm fair in
decades.

Every now and again I catch a little golf bug

I still dabble in golf-related activities
once in a blue moon. I wouldn't call it "getting
back into the game" since almost all of the action
is exclusively at a driving range where I'll stare
at a ball gracefully making its way across the sky
before settling 250 yards away from the tee area.
Sometimes, I'll pretend that is my ball, and not
the one that rolled to a stop 20-yards away and
printed with "no, ass, this one is yours".

It was 2007 the last time I played a real
course. It was one of those courses that actually
had grass everywhere and was designed for
people who not only know what a birdie is but
have actually gotten a few. I gave up after about
nine holes. My heart was not in it, and it got
annoying when I would tee up the ball and word
would go out to all ends of the course to watch
out (justified though that warning may have
been).

No worries. I will find other passions and diverse ways to spend money – I have always wanted a Volvo. If I am really lucky, one (new passion) will lead to another (foreign sedan). Ski jumping seems easy. Maybe, at the age of 40-something, I could be an Olympic ski jumper. It seems easy enough. Slide down hill, let momentum take you far. Next, sell the screenplay about my story ("He was a married father of two looking for inspiration. Then, he dared to soar.") Finally, buying a sensible Swedish car with a high safety rating and good resale value.

As a bonus, as a ski jumper I could still be a jokester, applying super glue to the final 5-yards of the ski jump during pre-lims. That would get my Wikipedia page one step closer to Hal's in terms of being interesting.

First Date: An Origin Story

"Love is the triumph of imagination over intelligence." - H.L. Mencken

Every couple has an origin story. The whole phenomenon has even taken over Hollywood. Between Marvel and G. I. Joe, we are learning about how even the most obscure characters got their start, even if they actually died four movies ago.

Our origin story, like many others, starts with online dating. I will not belabor the point – I will just stick to a few of the more unique aspects of the journey. Writing a profile, the initial email, etc. All of that is well-worn territory for humor columns.

So, I will skip that for the most part and just say these few things that eventually ended in a happy marriage:

The first steps

My profile picture was taken on my couch in my living room (in a 550 square foot apartment) fake talking on a nifty looking cell phone that I borrowed from a neighbor. I was going for the always-on-the-move go getter of Washington, DC lore. All it really got me was a date with a woman who did some sort of humanitarian work in Africa. Apparently, the chief of the local tribe made several requests to be intimate with her – something about tradition. My immature self was able to resist asking the "So....uhm...just one follow up to that story..."

question. Apparently, she was asked to leave that assignment early, so I assume that the chief was not successful (or was it – was that why she was asked to leave?). But that is not a hurdle that can really be cleared on assumption alone. She was on the traditional DC career track: spending way too much money on an education and then getting a job that paid – on a year-to-year grant that could dry up at a moment's notice – $21k per annum.

I also dated a woman who was on a slightly more realistic track: paying way too much money on education to, eventually, become a research doctor. Sometime in the next 15 years, she would earn enough to pay her student loans and splurge for a weekend trip to the beach. Her unique situation was that her focus area was degenerative brain diseases that eliminated the patient's inhibitions. Thus, her subjects were routinely trying to grab her. I am not a jealous man, but there is only so much I could take. I was not about to ask about Ronald's bowel movements in order to indirectly get to whether or not he copped a feel again.

As a quick side note, my first dip in the online dating pool came when I was living in Southern California. The woman I was chatting with said that her ideal first date was to sit together while the sun came up, facing the ocean, and absorbing the energy of the day. This must have been her first swing of the bat, because the sun rises in the east and the ocean is out west. The only thing we would be absorbing would be damaging UV rays on the backs of our necks.

A recalibration

With those efforts floundering I decided to change things up to better reflect who I truly was. My profile picture became a photoshopped version of me dunking on Michael Jordan. My "about me" was, more or less, true. Sure, there were a few white lies that led to slightly awkward conversations.

"You found John Wilkes Booth after he shot Lincoln? Hasn't he been dead for more than one hundred years?"

"Well, I didn't say I was the first to find him. I just went to his tomb – after Lincoln was assassinated – and boom! There he was. So, what I said was not inaccurate."

And:

"You say that you cured – in your words - 'ball cancer'. I've never read about that."

"Yes, terrible business, that. The doctor I was working with – Dr. I.P. Freely – was run off the road by one of Big Pharma's goons and all of our research was stolen."

Some women, including my now-wife, are suckers for a good I.P. Freely joke. And it is not like she is totally clean in all this. She claimed to like watching baseball but could hardly explain the difference between a suicide squeeze and a safety squeeze (I gave her a pass on double switching since we live in an American League city). We did the usual song and dance and decided to meet.

In person

I wore my nicest suit. That part was not a ruse. At the time I worked for the Federal Bureau of Investigation. While that sounds kind of cool on the surface, I was just starting out. My principal responsibilities included tying my own shoes, tying other people's shoes, and getting the newspaper for the big boss, with sections properly stacked precisely in the order he liked. One week, someone had already snarfed the ad insert to the supermarket he preferred. That was almost an unceremonious end to a short career.

Meanwhile, she clawed herself out of bed, threw on a t-shirt and jeans and met me at the restaurant we had previously agreed upon. I was certain that she needed an emergency IV, I just did not know if it was because she had been drinking all day or was just really sick. It turns out she was recovering from a weeklong flu but did not need the IV in the end.

126

We had chosen a place that was regionally famous for its crab cakes, and the night that we went there was crab cake special night. Even more crab in cake forms at a slightly reduced price. Being regionally famous for your crab cakes is no joke in the Baltimore area. To get that kind of rep, you have to produce a mighty good cake of crab. I figured that we would both get the special, but when she went to order, my date chose a club sandwich. What?

That is like going to Red Lobster during Endless Shrimp week and ordering the taco salad. Nothing against a taco salad, but they are finite. The shrimp are endless.

"Sir, I am not usually one to make recommendations – I am not paid nearly enough to care that much but...you could have ordered endless shrimp. Theoretically, you could have an infinite number of dead crustaceans. Instead, you ordered something that we – frankly – are not very good at. I mean, we're called 'Red Lobster'; most people tend to go the seafood route when they come here."

Nonetheless, her club sandwich came out, along with a server who wore a befuddled look on her face. The server set the stack of non-crab related product in front of my date, shrugged, and gave me my acclaimed crab cakes. It was a fine-looking sandwich, to be sure, six-inches tall and cut into quarters. What my date did not know was that I was going to have her eat the thing without any deconstruction. As an engineer by trade at the time, I figured that this would be a simple hurdle for her to clear. How wrong I was. Immediately, the torrent of lettuce, tomato, and other detritus fell onto the plate with the vigor of a summer thunderstorm.

Mayonnaise was everywhere. All was well, even though she was so distracted over how to get that into her mouth that she appeared to forget about the four toothpicks with colored plastic wrapped around their tops that had been lodged into each quarter of the sandwich.

The after-party

It was still early, so she asked if I wanted to continue the date.

"Sure," I replied, "What did you have in mind?"

"Have you ever been to a Wegman's?"

"I know what Wegman's is, but I have not yet been inside of one."

So, we went to a grocery store on our first date. In fairness to the good people at Wegman's, the store was very clean, and the selection was outstanding. I have never seen so much produce watered by some sort of automatic irrigation so frequently. Some aisles had so much

water that they might as well have been
hydroponic farms.

The seafood selection was also
impeccable. I am not sure I have seen fish
labeled as Dover sole in a grocery store in
Maryland before. I did not get anything since I
had no idea what other exciting plans she had -
the public library? and I didn't want anything
to go bad on my drive home. It turns out that she
did have something else planned, and it was so
horrific that I was scared even with all of my FBI
training (shoe tying): her one bedroom apartment
that had no roommates/witnesses. Here we were,
on our first date after having met online, she
looked like she was going to harvest an organ or
two to sell for heroin, and she was asking me to
go into a dark and empty apartment.

Curiosity got the best of judgement, and
in I went. If it was my time to depart this good
earth, at least it would make for an interesting
story at my funeral.

*"They found his body – totally stripped of any
useful organs – in the back of a Ford Bronco.
The cause of death was listed as 'asphyxiation by
tickling.' The coroner says that is fairly common,
as it preserves the organs as much as possible."*

I, obviously, survived – I even kept all of
my limbs and digits! And it wasn't what you

think, you cad! Get your mind out of the gutter. We just needed a place to chat that wasn't a local retailer. Perhaps less luckily, everything that happened in the apartment could have shone in a G-rated movie. Though this was in part because, her mother called twice to check on the situation, part of me was happy about the situation- It gave me the chance to yell for help if I needed to. I figured that they would not be in cahoots to kill me and sell of my body to Hong Kong-based surgeons. I mean, what are the odds that I would be targeted by a mother/daughter team of organ harvesters?

Marriage

So, here we are more than a decade later, happily married with two kids who seem relatively well-adjusted. It should be noted that she eventually got me back for the sandwich issue. On our wedding day she pretended that she could not hear the harpist switch songs to signal her entrance and walk down the aisle. The poor harpist just kept going. The bridesmaids got nervous. My groomsmen, always at the ready, tried to slip me a swig of whiskey.

But I knew the score.

Well played, sandwich face.

Video Games: The Digital Battles of our Lives

"We do not stop playing because we grow old. We grow old because we stop playing." - Benjamin Franklin

For better or for worse, video games are a part of our kids' social lives. Everyone plays them and to shield my kids from them would be folly at best and to disadvantage them socially at worst. At the same time, I can honestly say that the kids and I have bonded over playing them.

By the time the mid-80's had rolled around – when I had learned that my underpants shouldn't have cartoon characters on them – all the way through high school and college, I enjoyed playing video games. I was not so much into the more advanced games, the role-playing games, and the like. I was all-in on sports video games. I started with the Sega Master System classics, the uniquely named Great Baseball and Great Basketball. "Great" is a lofty way to describe those games, but they got the job done in the late-1980s. I moved onto the Sega Genesis and picked up Joe Montana Sports Talk Football II, where Joe would guide a nameless and faceless team (the game did not have the rights to actually use NFL team names) down the field to the sounds of groundbreaking sports commentary technology. "He...makes...the catch." It was also my entry point into the EA Sports games that had league rights and could use team nicknames. I should note that by "playing sports games" I mean taking advantage of the simplistic nature of the games during the PlayStation 2 era (1998ish-2002ish) that had just enough settings to tinker with and make ridiculously easy to obliterate any opponent in any sport that EA Sports stuck in front of me.

FIFA 2002 was a fun one. I would take Leeds United (they were still relevant and actually in the Premiership at the time) to dozens of undefeated seasons. Typically, we would end up with a goal differential of +14,452. Sometimes, I'd intentionally get a few red cards by slide tackling the goalie just to make the lads really work to earn their 22-1 win over Chelsea. Other times, I'd change it up and let some country that God forgot win the World Cup or would steer a plucky Norwegian club to Champions League glory. Rosenborg was relentless in its 15-0 thrashing of Real Madrid.

When it came time for the other football, Madden, I would make sure that the difficulty setting was on "Moron" and go nuts. The "Moron" setting ensures that an elderly cat at least 5 pounds north of obese and more interested in getting their next hit of catnip can win handily.

In these games, I'd win by ~90 points and ensure that the opposing team finished with negative total yards. Even though the players were nothing more than a series of zeros and ones, I still felt as though I broke their digital souls. I loved the canned animations that showed the QB getting frustrated after he was sacked for the 50th time. What did you expect, pal? A magical turn-around in the play of your offensive line?

Over time, games got more smarter (sic) and my Genghis Khan gene (isn't there some weird stat that says 98.99999% of all people are related to Khan and/or like Mongolian beef?) lost its proverbial mojo. A sense of video game ennui set in, and the various consoles made their way into storage to collect dust.

Back to the kids

During the time between my youthful dalliance with video games and the time that the kids were born and old enough, video games were pretty much left on the shelf. About two years ago, when the kids were ready, we dusted them off and my wife and I started them on Mario Kart and Wii Sports on the WiiU. This was a promising idea in spirit, but ultimately not very useful since we are the only people in the mid-Atlantic that own a WiiU.

Senior executives from Nintendo came to our house and begged us to be part of their new "See? Someone else actually bought this!" advertising campaign. Mario Kart was fun (more on that later) and the WiiU Sports package was amusing, even though that damn golf game had it in for me. No way those putts break that much.

Still, we moved on. With money burning holes in my pockets, and a genuine desire to expand the kids' horizons, we upgraded to an XBox1 and Star Wars Battlefront I. The boys are enamored with the Star Wars universe (even though I find the whole franchise tragically overrated). First person shooters are a thing, I guess, and it seemed like a safe entry to the genre for the kids. When a Storm Trooper gets shot, they just twitch a bit, fall down, and then the corpse magically disappears. No gore. I think that the after-action readout that counts "head shots" is a little much, however. I'd prefer "groin shots". If we are going to end the lives of an entire regiment of storm troopers, I think that imagining them going to Valhalla while clutching their hogs lightens the mood. It took some time to go through all of the various types of blasters and other implements of hog destruction, but the boys were vigilant and eventually got through them all.

Those games ran their course after a while (there are only so many different ways to off a stormtrooper) and then we went back to my strong suit growing up: sports games. It started with Madden 17 (why pay $999.99 for a game that is only slightly better than a game that costs as much as an old shoe?) and – wow! – that is one complicated game. For starters, all of the buttons on the controllers actually do something. And you can even set the prices on concessions at your stadium! How can I tutor my kids on ripping out the metaphorical heart of the game? Trying? Facing adversity? That's for suckers. What could I possibly do to even the odds? Of course, by "even the odds" I mean make it impossible for the team controlled by the computer to execute the most basic things, like typing their shoes. When I play the Cleveland Browns, I want them all to be in Velcro cleats.

The create-a-player era

The create-a-player function came to the rescue. That neat perk can make both super players and players so horrible that they couldn't even get drafted into the Army in 1967 during the Vietnam War.

We live in Howard County, MD, so the Ravens are our team. To start, we created B. McPoopsie, a 55-year-old running back who is 7' 400lbs with a rating of 99 in every category. Our QB is Chuck Weener, another 99-er who is 5' 6" and 160lbs. Offensive dominance was afoot. Yet, defensively, there was still a relatively even playing field. So, in a flash of brilliance, that I believe would have tucked in nicely with the 18th Century's Age of Enlightenment, we opted not to change the Ravens' defense. Rather, we ravaged the opposition's offense.

We decided on screwing with the Browns – I mean, why not? - and gave them an offensive line of players, all of whom were zeroed out on the relevant categories. Robert Griffin III's numbers (remember, this is 2017) dropped dramatically. The most "famous" of their line was B. Name (I got tired of naming all these schmucks), a 7' 160lbs center who struggled to bench press a Matchbox car.

But why stop there? With an abundance of time over the holiday break, we crippled the Browns' defense by sending them an array of pipsqueaks to try to deal with Weener and McPoopsie. "Awareness" appears to be one of the more critical attributes and zeroing that out lobotomizes the player to the point where they are only passively aware that a football game is even being played. If they do decide to run during a play, it is always in the wrong direction.

After establishing digital dominance over a game that is saying "I don't care – you bought me after all. EA got what it wanted," we decided to get silly. As a result, there are two new Ravens on the roster:

Q. Weasel is a massive punter that can kick the ball 18 miles. Occasionally, we will line up for a punt at the defense's 2-yard line to see if Weasel can punt it out of the stadium (he can). M. Fartsly is the worst kicker in recorded history, zeroed out in all categories. Fartsly, during a PAT, routinely kicks the ball into the holder. Right in his ass.

There we sit: a bunch of jolly idiots doing silly things and laughing so hard together that

Mommy cannot think straight even though she is in another room. It is just a few times a week, and I do not actually play – the boys alternate – but I am there with them and we...

...well, we laugh so hard that sometimes we have to take a potty time-out for fear that one of the boys will pee themselves the next time the Raven's holder takes another botched kick in the pooper.

FIFA was up next. It followed the same path as Madden: a brief introduction to figure out the controls and then it was off to Create-a-Player. Predictably, the beautiful game was infused with a series of international footballers with names like Farts Bigpoop, D.A. Hogg, the single-named Assman, and Zed Wank, the best goalkeeper the Earth has ever seen. Each had uniquely odd body shapes and all of the relevant traits were maxed out to 100. FIFA has so many traits that in the interest of time, I just altered the ones that were directly related to scoring goals or trucking weenies. I saw no need to adjust "sense of hair style" or "ability to pretend that they've been fouled". As a result, our squad was uglier, worse at acting, but technically superior to the opposition.

One new wrinkle was to adjust how hard the opposing team kicked the ball. This meant that we could make them tragically stupid and horribly inaccurate but with kicks that could top out at 600+ MPH. Even kick offs to start/restart play turned into masterpieces of ineptitude. A 6-inch love tap between two players standing arms' length apart turned into bullets that ended up 50 rows deep in the stands.

They were also sloth-like (by design), and even if the ball stayed in play, they could never make it to the ball in time before one of our players scooped it up. The Leadfeet United were also prime candidates for multiple slide tackle runs. Earning red cards was so easy that I was quickly reminded of the rule that says you forfeit the game if you get more than three. To date, that is the only way we have ever lost. Over time we would add NHL, NBA and MLB games to the list. Each new game followed a predictable – just still enjoyable – arc.

We did add two sports games with different angles. In the NASCAR game, there are no internal software blocks against driving the wrong direction. The worst the game will do to you as you rocket into oncoming traffic at 200+ MPH is to have your spotter radio "In case you didn't know it, you're driving in the wrong direction!" right before impact. Flips, cartwheels, and good air get applause, but the real cheers are reserved for when a car goes careening into the grandstand packed with digital fans drinking digital Bud Lights.

In our other game that deviates from the norm, golf, you really can't do too much with the player – aside from dressing them in obnoxious golf clothes – but you can alter the courses any way you want. You do not, for example, need water in play to put an oil tanker in the middle of the 7th hole at the Players Championship. There is something appealing about hitting your approach shot from the deck of a large ocean-going vessel. Even more fun, you can place all sorts of wildlife anywhere you like. For some reason, anytime these wimpy animals get hit by a golf ball, they fall over dead. Even if it is just a putt.

This is especially funny in two places on the course. At the tee, you can put a large, endangered species of African elephant right in front of the tee, giving you the chance to give it a good old whack with your driver. Then, on the green, you can surround the hole with nine reindeer. To make it in, you must kill Santa's sled team!

Head-to-head action

You may have noticed that there is a lot of collaborative language here. "We" and "Our" and the like. This is because my wife and I limit the head-to-head stuff. These games are fickle, and these boys are competitive enough without some computer processor deciding whether or not a cluster of pixels catches another cluster of pixels. We certainly don't shy the kids away from competition in other arenas (board games, sports, etc.) but if we can choose our battles and not fan the flames of a particularly random acting ember, so much the better. They will have plenty of time to cuss about "getting robbed" when playing against their friends in college.

I am not sure what is next for the XBox. I would like to push back on things like Call of Duty for as long as possible, but we are running out of sports games. Even if there was an EA Sports Handball game, I doubt the boys would really get that into it. Maybe there is a game comparable to Legends of Zelda or Metroid or something. Shinobi would work. I'll stop before I date myself any more than I already have...

The karts of Mario and friends

Earlier in this chapter I mentioned Mario Kart. This is one game that is completely alien to me - nothing of the sort existed in my childhood – but it simply must be addressed. We have the 8th iteration. It is actually pretty neat, so I figured to tell you everything you will ever need to know about it since 1) you will never play it and 2) a Nintendo anything is about as relevant today as a VCR. My kids, however, have become obsessed with it, and with using the online worldwide racing feature. It is one of the only games we let them play online. There is no real reason why, except that they seem less likely to be mad losing to a 30-year-old living in his/her parent's basement in Inchon, South Korea than they are to that same person in Madden

So, in case this insidious force knocks on your door (possibly looking like a vagrant panhandler), here are a few things to know. This will seem rather esoteric at first – a gentle ribbing of a particular game that most kids would not admit to playing – but stick with me. Some video game themes can apply to a lot of different things in life. Mostly, how paying close attention to absurdities can waste a ton of valuable time.

The characters are odd (aside from the old stand-bys that date back to the 80's). Holy cow. Who produced this menagerie?! Skeletal turtle-ish things with large burning shells are on the same selectable roster as Baby Princess Peach. One version of Mario looks like he is made from liquid metal, like the bad robot in Terminator 2. If this guy stabs another competitor in the head with a metal spike, I am turning the game off immediately--Luigi deserves better. Dry Bowser is the skeletal remains of one of the live characters; that makes sense. I get that there is a Nintendo canon, and that many of these characters have been around for decades. The Link character is definitely a fan favorite in our house. The boys call him "Hog Man" because he whips out his sword anytime he does a jump. The sword is previously hidden from view and the jump makes Hog Man reach into his pants – precisely where the hog would be – and whip out the steel phallic object in triumph.

I also think it is neat that some un-Mario characters make it into the game. Still, having 20+ characters that range from babies with pacifiers to metal cartoon characters that look straight out of the hit movie franchise of Terminator seems odd.

The carts (or, "karts") are another area in the game where the selections run the gamut from practical to absurd. The karts are not bound to any character, so an enormous Donkey Kong can ride a tiny motorcycle designed for a baby Toad. Some designs just don't make any sense at all. One of the choices is a weird-ass thing that more closely resembles a horse on a carousel than anything you would find on a racetrack. It even bobs up and down, even when not moving forward/backward.

The real problem, however, is not with how strange these things are. It is that there are so many of them, each with statistical scores in several performance categories. There are so many choices that the kids will pour over the stats for minutes trying to figure out if the Mario version of the T-1000 should choose this kart over that kart.

To make matters worse, the kids can select from any number of tires, and gliders.

"Tires" made of wood don't really seem to go with a glider that looks like a fire breathing dragon.

Stats be damned

Despite the best efforts of some overworked and underpaid software engineer to properly code in the drag coefficient of a beach umbrella glider, the stats don't matter. Instead of wasting 20+ minutes comparing tires, the player is well-served to just pick anything and get on with it already. Choose a cup (a series of four races) and finally get driving.

In Mario Kart, one of the rewards you can pick up while racing is a mushroom that makes you go faster. The only thing that would be more apt in terms of discussing the course design would be a marijuana leaf. Cuz man, those things (the courses) are weird. Some courses start underwater. Given the organization incumbent with getting 12 karts in line to start a meaningless race, this seems dodgy. How are these guys breathing? They clearly have no additional devices that would give respiratory assistance. One course even has you drive IN OUTER SPACE without appropriate protection. The list could go on – almost every course has several elements that violate the basic tenets of science. In the ice course, your racer plunges into freezing water, seemingly immune to the effects of hypothermia. Another course is made entirely out of candy. I don't even know where to start with that. And it goes on.

Over the last few months, I have seen more Mario Kart 8 than I would care to. If MK8 somehow adversely affected my cardiovascular system, I would be dead. The kids love it though. And, my wife and I do not let them have any more than a few races a day (we would not want to run the risk of messing with their cardiovascular health; or teach them that icy water is safe.). So, they relish in picking their tragically absurd characters, their karts, tires, and gliders, none of which makes even the slightest difference in terms of the outcome of the race. Then, they will gleefully career around Bowser's Castle for the 875th time, trying to be better than some Belgian person who, based on his cumulative score, plays way too much. They will also high-five and congratulate each other. Sometimes, they will even hug after a particularly good race that featured mind-numbingly obnoxious crimes against physics.

Mario Kart 8 is silly. It is, however, not violent. It gives the boys a fun outlet to pick their karts and whatnot and have an enjoyable time. We do not rely on Mario Kart 8 or sports games to occupy our kids, but we do use the good ones – in moderation – to have some fun, throw dead turtle's shells at each other, and take a break from academics. Plus, it can lead to conversation like this:

"Dad, I dreamt I was that weird elf thing riding a purple dot manatee that had off-road tires for flippers and that had a glider that looked like a large bat."

"No son, you weren't dreaming. You just missed your nap before starting to play Mario Kart 8 again..."

Our American Family Vacation Experience

"Educating the mind without educating the heart is no education at all" - Aristotle

We are lucky enough to be able to take a family vacation every summer. Typically, we spend a week at a beachfront condominium in North Myrtle Beach, SC. Since we live in Central Maryland, we have to drive between 9-10 hours to get from Point A to Point B vacation. Regrettably, this takes us down Interstate 95, which is one of the heaviest traffic corridors in all the land. Of course, the commute is more than worth the headache. Summer vacation is a wonderful time to be caged in a 34 sq ft condo with my family. This allows for the kids to have more hours than usual using technology (TV, video games, etc.) in between playing in the ocean, eating out 473% more than usual, and trying to avoid third-degree burns from private beach firework "displays". One year, our beach vacation coincided with the July 4th holiday, and we did not get more than three hours of sleep each night. I cannot begin to imagine how much money literally went up in smoke 100' above the Atlantic Ocean.

The vacation commutes

But back to the drive for a second. As mentioned, this is one of the most used stretches of interstate in America, and retailers pay top dollar to be within sight of all the cars that are slowly crawling along at 20-30 miles per hour. It is uncanny how many mega-car dealerships are visible from I-95 in Maryland, Virginia, and North Carolina. These places have car lots that measure in square miles. Sometimes there are two or three dealerships in a row – you can run a full marathon around them and see nothing but "great summer close-out deals." On aggregate, this land of instant rebates and no cash down, is the size of all of Rhode Island and Hartford, CT. Also, it should be noted, that Rhode Island is not an island.

Furthermore, the Lumen output of these crimes against the eye dwarfs, in one hour, the entire annual electrical output of North Korea and Bhutan COMBINED. And the lights are on at 4AM! (We leave tragically early to beat summer traffic in Virginia, which is a holy mess.) I am here to tell you: never has someone driving on an interstate at 4AM seen a Nissan dealership in Maryland and thought "You know, when we get back from our week-long vacation, we'll have to check that joint out. I have heard a lot of great things about the new Rogue."

Continuing the superfluous light theme, Virginia has a lot of needless illumination in the form of pole lights. Sure, that is a great idea for tricky intersections, but a light every ten yards on a straight and level HOV lane being used by two people at 5:30 AM is folly. Modern headlights and the local geography have eliminated the need for such aggressive illumination.

Our annual sojourn takes us past dozens of rest stops. Over the years, thanks to two kids who cannot coordinate their bladder functions, we have been to most of them. I will not revisit the hack jokes about their cleanliness, but I will say this about that: I am glad that my kids and I can stand up. As for my wife? My policy is to look at her ghost-white face and keep my mouth shut. On the plus side, it is fun to see the people pull in who clearly, as the exit to the previous rest stop zoomed by, thought: "Eh, no matter – I can make it another 25 miles!"

Once we leave Virginia, we hit North Carolina, which is practically another country. West Virginia and North Carolina are cousins. There is some weird stuff that goes on there. Last year I happened to notice that a road sign in the median had been blasted by a shot gun. I just figured it was a one-off. This year, I was on the prowl and saw ~10 more. Seriously, how does this happen? "We're getting near the sign for exit 165, JimBob. Lock and load!" In fairness to the great state of North Carolina, which has seen fit to not replace these signs, they are still legible.

Just before transitioning from North to South Carolina, we hop off the interstate and wind our way to the Atlantic coast by way of a series of well-maintained backroads. The views are exquisite Non-stop swampland replete with floating dead trees for miles and miles. Sometimes, you will get lucky and pass a tree that is only mostly dead and still vertical.

The condominium

In time, the land becomes more welcoming. The final direction – turn at the giant Wal-Mart – gets us to our condominium. It takes an hour or so to unpack (and to wait for the grocery delivery service) and then we can immerse ourselves in our temporary beach community. We kill a good bit of time sorting through the laundry and pulling out all the little toys/game tokens that spilled out of their containers during the drive.

Our place is a sturdy joint – four strong walls, and a ceiling that could probably survive 25.1 seconds of jack hammering. The locks are nice and tough to manage (we have keys and only succeed on the first attempt 50% of the time). That's not to say we stay in a bad area – far from it – it is just that all the doors look the same, and this is a strange setting for most vacationers. I prefer an annoyingly sturdy lock to ensure that I do not encounter a random – and possibly inebriated – person at 3:00 in the morning. The parking situation is different but tolerable.

At home in Maryland, when I get home from picking up dinner from Wendy's, I can park in my driveway, and stroll over relatively flat ground to get to my door. It takes 4 calories to haul in a bag full of 18,000 calories (which would require about 1440 minutes of running to burn off). Furthermore, I am out of a climate-controlled environment for 30 seconds or so.

At the condo? The parking lot is a sea of asphalt that the sun has heated to roughly 432 degrees Kelvin. In fairness, this has some physical fitness benefits. I must park in a spot that is 50 yards from the building and pass a group of people who are – inexplicably – drinking beers next to their small cluster of Ford F-150s. Then I have to slog my sack of junior bacon cheeseburgers up a series of steps, one of which – and I can never remember which one until it is too late – has a protruding rusty nail.

Get your tetanus shots, kids.

During our most recent vacation, thanks to a larger vehicle, we packed more than usual in order to avoid having to go to a retail store and pick up emergency AA batteries for an overused Xbox1 controller. Thus, we tried to cram a week's worth of supplies (in addition to the groceries we had delivered) into a space roughly the size of a bathroom stall at Burger King.

Getting everything in and stowed away is a delicate dance fit for Broadway. The level of choreography employed by my wife is elite. Of course, even the best-laid plans can falter. Before the tasks are all complete, she has ordered the rest of us to the balcony to get us out of her hair.

Living in a condo for seven days is a hilarious experience in sociology. Even though we go to the same place each year, the neighbors are always different. Our unit is on the first floor (which is really the second level; the first level is reserved for wayward ocean water during hurricanes. It is always exciting to learn about our week-long neighbors. The first night of the most recent vacation iteration, we learned that the people above us are actually a family of kangaroos. There is simply no other way – I checked with NASA – that a human could jump that much and run that loudly for that long.

Rutherford Honwickly, who holds a Ph.D. in Hopping Mammals, and I briefly considered a herd of elephants, but quickly ruled that out due to spatial constraints.

At least they are healthy. If they had step/jump-counters, it would return a daily number of steps/jumps of 1.76 million. That equals 72,916.66667 per hour. I checked.

The second day, we learned that the laundry washer in the unit two floors directly above us had suffered a catastrophic failure. The fellow who was up there came down to warn us of an incoming deluge. Luckily, it never came – just a few drops in our utility room – but while waiting I did some research. According to explodinglaundry.com, the industry experts, the leading cause of exploding washers that are within 3.2km of a beach, is:

"a self-destruct mechanism that kicks in when the washer must run its 45th load of sandy swim trunks in less than 24 hours."

Apparently, the guy is the owner of the unit, and had to lug the doomed machine down three floors. Then, he had to hoist a new machine up those same sets of stairs (the ones with the random rusty nail).

I would have loved to help even though the heat and humidity would wither most species of camels, but...social distancing and all that.

Team Kangaroo's step counter would dwarf this guy's daily total. But he burned more calories in one day than Lance Armstrong did in his cycling career.

Being in the midst of COVID-related restrictions, we were able to be safe and stay away from our neighbors. The facility was roughly 25% full, and the beach had been a ghost town. Still, there are some things we learned about the (few) people around us.

One fellow is a smoker. Smoking, by all objective measures, is an unhealthy habit. I can't throw stones though. I have an unhealthy habit: following the Baltimore Orioles. Nonetheless, even when baseball season is actually a thing, I do not spend my entire day on my addiction, trying to explain why the O's team ERA is higher than 50.

This guy smokes all day. From the time we walk out onto the balcony to see the sunrise, to well after the random fireworks start at night, the dude is puffing on something (he goes back and forth between cigs and cigars).

Smokey, if he had a fitness tracker, which is highly unlikely, would only register the total distance to/from the bathroom multiplied by the number of times he used the can.

Beach traditions

Still, even with the constant threat from second-hand smoke and the ever-present specter of COVID, we were able to enjoy some of the more meaningful activities. Flying a kite is timeless, and is a family tradition. The boys love flying their kites. Their kite flying strategies are hilariously dichotomous, and I swear watching them is just as healthy as running a 10k.

I guess I am halfway "home" in terms of age if you believe current life-expectancy projections. If I am being honest, probably more than halfway if you knock off a few years due to my love of buffalo wings, nacho cheese, and not running. However, I will gladly run up and down a beach with a kite, trying to give it enough upward thrust to gain elevation even while it is just bouncing along through the sand. Any year I can still do that is a good year. Especially if the damn thing gets into the air. If/when it comes to pass that I cannot maintain enough velocity for a long enough period of time, I guess I can always rent a bike. I would rather not play that card anytime soon though, or as anything but a last resort.

My youngest son's kite is shaped like an F-117 fighter/bomber. This is wonderfully appropriate. He eschews the time honored "Gentle Flight" school of thought in favor of the new age "Dive Bomb" sect. He is not happy unless someone is looking at his kite with an elevated blood pressure.

He will twist his arms in a most melodious way – like a symphonic conductor – to ensure that nothing on the beach is safe. As long as something is in the range of this aerial menace (as dictated by the length of the kite string), it is not safe.

Beach-side trash cans/recycling bins? You are cooked. Relatively low-flying seagulls are also in play. Since Youngest's targeting is unintentional and indiscriminate, even the guy combing the beach with his metal detector might catch a kite in his noggin.

Quick aside: I have been going to the beach for 37 years. I have never seen a metal detector guy score a win. That is, unless you count a rusty Dos Equis bottle cap from 1992 as a win. The same can be said for the sunset shore fishers. No fish, 3+ decades. Give up; our finned friends are onto you.

My oldest son's strategy is far more ambitious. He will go to the ends of the Earth to ensure that he has the highest kite in sight. While I appreciate his dedication to the craft, his only real competition is his brother, whose kite just took out a vacant lifeguard stand.

So, while Youngest is trying to fish his kite out of a sand dune after a wayward attempt to strike the wood box that stores the rental umbrellas overnight, Oldest has turned his eyes towards getting his kite higher than our condominium (he has succeeded several times). Perspective is a funny thing, and from the sand it can look like the kite could easily sail over the building. But – thanks to the limited amount of string - it can't. It would lodge itself in a third-floor balcony, taking out a wine cooler or two.

My wife is a math teacher and could probably explain the situation using some witchcraft called trigonometry. We just give him the win and spare him the high school math lesson.

On it goes – flying a kite is tremendous fun. Especially when it is time to reel the kite in for the night. Those last several yards are very unpredictable, as chaotic air flows wreak havoc on the kite pilot. Kite flying also has the benefit of not making my knees ache. Unlike yoga, Namaste, whole-of-body pain.

While on vacation, we obviously play in the ocean (more on that later). We have an annual tradition of making sandcastles with several layers of defense to keep the rising ocean at bay as long as possible. My youngest is a bit of a pessimist. He flees for another activity as soon as the first water touches the outermost wall.

We will also go for family walks and toss the football around. The football sessions are especially fun. I will throw to the kids and, at their request, lead them right into a wave. If I am lucky, it will be the closest they ever get to getting laid out by a cornerback. These things do make me ache in places I did not ache a decade ago. It is all worth it – seeing their joy when we are all out there as a family.

Maybe that benefit will have enough of a positive therapeutic effect to outweigh the buffalo-wing-assisted life-expectancy challenge.

Fitness at the beach

Along those lines, Vacation is a great time to start getting back into shape. With it being summer, I will have the time to keep up the momentum. At home, I have been running (well, plodding, if I am being honest), messing with gravity (lifting weights), and using a stationary bike. I have also started to take supplements like "vitamins" and "minerals."

I am nearly 40, and I can afford to use excuses like "It is vacation" or "That blue jay is looking at me funny" to get out of exercise. It is time to get myself ready for retirement so I can live as many days as possible doing crossword puzzles, watching golf, and complaining about the weather (even though I never have to actually go outdoors). Plus, I will want to keep up with my wife (within reason). When we go to the mailbox – assuming mail still exists – I want to be able to make it each way with having to only take one break.

The family beach vacation offers whole new ways to work out new groups of muscles that were not covered by the home routine. This makes the muscles, and possibly the colon, angry.

I hit the ground running, so-to-speak. Unloading the large vehicle, we crammed with more material than was needed for D-Day is tough. Even though I only have to slog up around 20 stairs, my wife is fond of packing as much as possible into every container. The suspension on our 2019 minivan looks like it has circumnavigated the globe four times.

She knows she will not have to carry it up to the condo.

The local seagulls are wise. They know that when they see someone like me start to unpack it will be a long and agonizing process. They use – best I figure – seagull cellphones to call their buddies. Within short order, a large group of them will have stopped picking at whatever carryout leftovers were in the dumpsters and lined up on the fence at the end of the lot to watch me sweat and listen to me swear.

But that is just the beginning

Within minutes of arriving/unpacking, after an 8+ hour drive that started at 4 AM, the boys want to get in the ocean. Even walking to the beach is tough. Remember, I've just moved 98 metric tons of freight from the cargo ship USS Pacifica. Waddling through the soft sand that is hotter than sauce made from ghost peppers confirmed what I knew was coming: my legs, already bothered by my poor life decisions, would go into full revolt. Fortunately, this limb-uppityness would give me an excuse to not run while the rest of me tamped down the Great Quad Rebellion of 2020.

My kids are like large fish or small marine mammals – take your pick. I guess the youngest would be like a carp, and the oldest would be more of an undersized yellow-fin tuna. That's just a guess though – I am not an ichthyologist. My estimations may be off a bit.

The point is that they are constantly in the water, following directions roughly 34.99% of the time. So, I am also constantly in the water. The kids aren't the type who just lazily float out past the breakers. They keep a frenetic pace that includes body surfing, boogie boarding, and skim boarding. Even getting to/from parent-mandated breaks is an effort since they insist on sprinting to/from the ocean. Admittedly, the surf there is not as gnarly as Ocean City, MD, where

I grew up, but it is still an ocean and danger still lurks. The boys are very safe, but waves are funny things, and Youngest occasionally needs to be plucked from the roiling surf.

As he increases in mass year-to-year, it increases the impact on my lower back muscles. And those muscles have no desire to be impacted at all. Picking up a wounded shrew to nurse it back to health is an effort these days.

Upper body, lower back, glutes, and cardio: all rolled into several two-hour sessions punctuated by 15-minute breaks, five of which are spent repeating "We'll go back in soon."

Even though I joked about it earlier, I will still force myself to run at least once each vacation. Running is the one thing that I can do at the beach that mirrors my home routine. When General Left Calf or the Council of Quads allow me to, I will get back at it. The only problem is that, given the tide schedule for this particular week, I'll be confined to loose sand (it will be high tide, or close to it, during peak running time). I think I'll turn the fitness tracker off for those jaunts. No need to get demoralized to the point where I'll binge-hire four personal trainers.

There is one fitness/health benefit to beach week that requires no effort: being in the sun. In 48 hours, I absorb more Vitamin D than I had in the last 48 days.

Arriving back home

The last hurrah of vacation is the first dinner back home. The drive back takes significantly longer since we hit Virginia and Washington, DC later in the day, when it takes hours to go three miles. By the time we get home and unpack only that which is essential to remove from the van, all we want to do is put something – anything – into our stomachs. We are very limited in terms of ingredients, relying on foods that could make it more-or-less unrefrigerated in a car for 12+ hours and foods that have been in our freezer for God only knows how long. Every year seems to feature chicken patties as the "main course".

Frozen chicken patties are curious things. First, are they really chicken? I've seen chickens before, both live and butterflied (among other forms of chicken), and no part of them resembles a thin disc that can be excised for human consumption. I assume that the manufacturing process involves a $1.3 million industrial grade grinding machine, and unused fruit cake from the previous year's holiday season (to ensure a sufficient level of rigidity).

The second question is about the thin layer of orange stuff that has been applied to the "chicken." They can't possibly be breadcrumbs. No breadcrumb is that thin – I even asked the National Breadcrumb Institute for confirmation. The manufacturers of the patty must be using lab-created particles to encircle the "chicken" to make sure that the souls of the ground-up birds do not escape. The only bonus they add is the fact that they help bind whatever sauces happen to be in the fridge.

After heating the patty to a level that raised the Gastro-Intestinal Threat Level from "Certain Doom" to "Make Sure you Have Enough TP", we are left with an entree of flavorless "chicken" ensconced in scientifically created "breadcrumbs". Clearly, we need to take additional steps to make this crime against nature more palatable.

So, we do what any good American would: we toss that poultry hockey puck in between two slices of white bread. Still, the abomination that we have in front of us is only slightly more appealing than the week-old cucumber that camped out in the veggie drawer and looked as though it had been pooped out by someone who ate too many vegetables. More needs to be done.

Things in our refrigerator are constantly moved around, mostly to make space for new items. For example, a bottle of ranch dressing can find itself behind a four-gallon jug of tomato juice. Years later, even more shuffling will reveal its sad corpse, a monument to what could have been, topped with a cap covered in gobs of half-solid dressing. We have multiple copies of the same condiment in our fridge, having unknowingly re-purchased what we already had in stock.

When you have eight bottles of mustard to choose from, all of which look the same, it is key to select the freshest one. Given that the patty meal is already a significant threat to physical well-being, selecting a jug of mayo that had been purchased during the Obama administration would further compound the issue.

Nonetheless, after a careful examination of the digitally printed expiration dates (that seem to be intentionally obfuscated), we are in business. After a robust application of questionably fresh mayo, mustard, ketchup, fermented tomato juice, and others, a sandwich is ready. The only item I am supremely comfortable with is the pickle. Those things never go bad.

The final task is to come up with a side dish. This was key – we have to offset the fresh hell that is the Frankenstein chicken sandwich. We have lettuce - or at least something leafy and kind of green that could pass for lettuce if the lights went out. The kids add on some of the poop cucumber (I abstain), and our side is a "salad" of lettuce and a poopcumber.

After consuming food that I strongly suspect I will be re-introduced to before long, it was time to ensure that the bathroom was stocked with a sufficient amount of toilet paper. Then, collapse and pretend that I do not have to go back to work for three more weeks.

Fitness Part II – The Family Team Events

"Alone, we can do so little; together we can do so much." - Helen Keller

Yard Fun

Our family yard is modestly sized, but it does not stop us from having some fun using it. The property is about a quarter of an acre with a plot of public land behind it. Ringed in mature trees, it gives good shade in the summer which is useful for temperature management but dreadful for maintaining a lush bed of grass.

Mostly, the boys like to play soccer or football. We have a small goal that the kids sometimes hit, which gives them a point and saves me from having to retrieve the ball from the neighbor's yard. Again. Sometimes, we will toss baseball into the mix, but the elevated nature of a batted ball means that even a well-placed soccer goal will not prevent the ball from landing in someone else's realm. For this reason, we only use those tee balls that are baseball sized but about as hard as a water balloon.

When our youngest is batting, it is fun to gamble over which yard the ball will come to a stop in. There are really only three yards in play. He's magically managed to reach a fourth. And of course, he doesn't much care about the difference between fair and foul.

Closeness

"Closeness" could refer, in a sappy manner, to how close our family is when we are in the yard. Pshaw. Here, it is all about how close our yard is – obviously – to our house. Until the boys are too big to use the yard, all I must do to access it is open a door and cross a 20-foot patio. No driving, no excessive walking. Certainly, no talking to the unsavory childless people who hang out at playgrounds.

Crossing the patio does have its peril. Well, "perils". In order to get across, you must pass the hot tub with the factory setting of bellowing "None shall pass!" anytime someone draws near. "I had to get in sweetheart. The tub made me!" I could be wearing sweatpants and a Baltimore Orioles hoodie that is slightly too small for me, and still be tempted to hop in for a nice soak.

Closeness also refers to the confines of the yard, which means I have considerably less running to do. The boundaries are such that a weak pass from a small rodent could kick/throw the ball out of bounds, hitting a bush, tree, or soccer goal and stopping it.

The nearest regulation field is at the local elementary school and doubles as the seasonal home to roughly 562 geese. If we were to rely on that field, in addition to me becoming horribly winded, the entire family would have to go into a rigorous de-goosepoop protocol. We've been down that road before: "Mommy! Stop! You are just scrubbing bone!"

It is best to either just wait until they leave or seed the fields with whatever makes a goose constipated and pray that you aren't in the flight path when they all take off and jettison the excess weight that has built up.

The uniforms

Regardless of the sport, Youngest wears his Juventus kit. (As a word nerd, I think that is funny, since Juventus traces back to the Latin word for youth.) This jersey, shorts, and socks combo are hilariously threadbare. I have concert t-shirts from the mid-1990s that are in better shape. Admittedly, I do not have much occasion to wear a Third Eye Blind shirt, but still...

Oldest typically wears a tank top, paying homage to his suburban Maryland roots, and loose shorts. My wife wears an assortment of yoga/workout attire, paying homage to her suburban Maryland mom status.

I wear a Speedo and a Cal Ripken Jr. shirt.

Kidding.

Pride in ownership

The boys have really started to pay
attention to the yard's upkeep – they seriously
enjoy our time out there. – and their mommy's –
joy in gardening, but now they are more into the
more mundane yard-related chores. Oldest can
mow the lawn on his own. Youngest can...use
the mower to cut tragically irregular swaths into
the grass, and possibly threaten the lives of the
family of groundhogs that live nearby. But he
tries.

Weed whacking is still a lost art to them,
but my wife and I enjoy a good amount of
offspring support when it is time to rake the
leaves. This is helpful since we get a ton of
leaves. So many leaves fall from our trees that
we cannot even take part in the suburban
tradition of just letting them blow into a
neighbor's yard.

They both like to water the yard with the
sprinkler. However, they also see fit to romp
around over the increasingly wet, and soft, soil.
This, of course, is antithetical to the point. We
have precious few blades of grass. The Maryland
summer will take most of the blades' lives,
especially with the excessive playing of both
types of football. Yet...

...joy, jumping, running, and laughing all seem
to be worth it. At least for us. Maybe not so
much for the grass that must watch its brethren

get stomped into oblivion every summer. At least when the snow falls, they cannot see the horrors.

Thanks for taking one for the team, Yard.

Street Hockey

With our yard in shambles, we needed a new arena in which to strive for athletic dominance.

So, here is a good story about trying to exercise: I fell on my ass. On something harder than chopped up grass. That pretty much sums it up.

It was a beautiful day in Central Maryland – sunny, upper-70s, light breeze, etc. – in short, the perfect day to head out and try to get moving. Our yard had recently been taking quite a beating, so I figured to give something else a try. In my youth, I was an avid street hockey player. For some reason, my only real athletic talent came in the form of an esoteric sport that had a participation rate of about .003% of kids my age in Harford County.

I had previously assembled all the equipment necessary for a game – skates, sticks, helmets, a ball, etc.

Things got off to a rocky start when my wife tried to put on her 20-year-old skates. Old Man Time kept up his winning streak, and the

172

plastic shattered into dozens of pieces when she
tried to secure the skates to her feet. In less than
2-minutes time, we were already down one
skater and facing an entire game where one team
had a power play advantage.

No worries. I was an excellent
defenseman – albeit undersized – back in my
day. And it was a little bit of insurance in terms
of injury prevention. My wife's counter-falling
strategy is less "consolidate physical mass over a
crucial point and regain balance" and more "flail
arms in such a manner that crashing down is
exponentially more likely". Even a well-fitting
helmet would struggle to dampen the impact as
she crashed to the ground yelping like a squirrel
with a sprained ankle.

I put my skates on – the idea was to skate
up to the lot while the boys walked to put on
their skates upon arrival – and made it around
five feet before...

...you guessed it; I fell on my ass.

It was a poorly conceived idea from the
start. Skating uses muscles that had lain dormant
for decades. Assuming that I made it the .5 miles
to the lot without shredding a ligament or two, I
would be a tired and sweaty mess. Of course, it
never got to that point. I struck out, skates nice
and tight on my ankles, down the driveway. I

was still slightly distracted by the structural collapse of my wife's skates and ran into a group of spiky balls that had pooled near one of the seams in the concrete. "Spiky balls" are the product of a tree here in Central Maryland that are used for reproduction. They are ~1-2" in diameter, harder than a lump of diamond, and fall from the trees by the hundreds. For some reason, the planners of my community decided to curse us all by planting dozens of these diamond-hard seed-pod excreting menaces around the neighborhood. It would have been less annoying if the planners had seeded the area with man-eating tigers who had been genetically engineered to be ever more lethal and even more resistant to anti-tiger bullets.

My progress was immediately halted by the spiky ball convention being held in my driveway. Instantly, the bottom half of my body stopped dead. The upper part continued to go forward until my brain issued the command for an aggressive counter-correction backwards which, within seconds, forcibly dropped me on my rear end. The pain was instant. I screamed in agony as my butt bone registered its displeasure at what had just happened. I rolled over to my stomach – and a pack of spikey balls – to continue wiggling.

Ever the Warrior

Nonetheless, we still walked up to the lot.
I am a hockey player, after all. It is a moral
imperative to play through the pain. The boys
put on their skates and practiced skating.
Thankfully, they did not take after their father,
and managed to stay upright and ouchie free.
After a spell, we broke out the sticks and the ball
and played some hockey – boys on skates, mom
and hurt-butt dad on foot.

My ass started to hurt more and more,
with achiness drifting down my legs and up my
spine. At one point, I winged a wrist shot at one
of the boys. Like any normal father looking for
athletic glory wherever he can find it, I should
have had a euphoric reaction to scoring on two
kids playing street hockey for the first time.
Instead, I felt a bowel rattling shot of pain.
Quickly assessing that I was still roughly .5
miles away from my house, I decided that it was
time to sound the call for retreat and return to my
soft sofa, impeccably placed in front of a TV.
Actually, we have several soft sofas in front of
TVs to choose from. My wife is an expert at
home furnishing, and probably anticipated that
my clumsiness would lead to a need for multiple
sofas. I have, for example, fallen down the stairs
twice when our cats showed an unnecessary level
of interest in what I was taking to the basement.

It was fun, and the boys expressed a strong desire to play more street hockey (which, given my status at the time in terms of ass-pain, sent another shot of pain through my torso).

Never the Warrior

Once home, I settled into a relatively pain-free position on the couch. My wife and the boys wrapped up the day's play time by chewing up the yard like how an aggressive puppy chews up a car battery – which is exactly what I had hoped to avoid. There was a very positive development, however. After they wrapped up, my oldest on his own, mowed all seven blades of grass that were once part of a magnificent lawn. This was huge. It meant that I would soon forget what our lawn mower even looked like. He even did a pretty good job and can be forgiven for mowing the same swath of land 20-22 times. It was his first time. He just needed to get into a rhythm.

As minutes passed into hours, the ass pain continued to grow. My body switched into its default setting: Full Wuss. I asked the boys to do everything for me. They even retrieved an ice pack to put on my lower back. I considered having them administer CPR to me, so my heart did not have to beat on its own.

I have a fitness app on my phone that tracks the number of steps I take each day. Yesterday, as I went into a full sedentary state, it actually started docking me steps that I had previously taken. When it did not stop at zero and drifted into negative steps/distance, I thought I might have come up with a plan to travel back in time. I was immortal! But I guess that is really how it all works.

Today, Ass Injury +1; I still cannot bend over. Sitting is tough and walking is a nightmare.

I will power through

The best part of being a melodramatic wuss with a total aversion to pain is that I can tolerate sitting on my (wounded) ass for as long as it takes to heal.

Doctor: "Don't rush it and try not to do too much too soon."

Me: "That is not an issue, hoss."

Football

After the first bout with street hockey, it was time to take a little break from the kind of sports that could further damage my poor rump. Thus, we decided to start our own football league. And did we ever!

The NFL should be worried – while they are still a few months away from getting back onto the field, the Daddy/Buddy/Mommy Football League (DBMFL) is into its third week of operation. Our attendance is skyrocketing. At our last game, a guy showed up to DBMFL Stadium (soccer field at local elementary school) and tried to fly a kite that was roughly the size of an 8.5″ by 11″ piece of paper, in a light breeze from the northwest. After consistently, and predictably, failing, he just sat on a hill and watched us from around 100 yards away. I'm glad that all was not lost for the poor fellow, but I question the sanity of a grown man who takes a kite – by himself – that is doomed from the start.

How Our Football League Works

The DBMFL is structured a little (read: a lot) differently. We only have 1.5 teams. To make things a little more even, and to satisfy my urge to minimalize physical activity, I play QB all the time. When the boys are on offense, I'm the QB and my wife defends both kids. This might seem tragically unfair, but the kids' WR corps is…lacking (there is nothing wrong with the QB play). And, thanks to social distancing, we had to suspend our first-year player draft.

When my wife and I are on offense, we will alternate QB responsibilities. Though when she gets the snap, it is technically a wildcat formation (the running back lining up at the quarterback position). In this phase, the game set-up is a more traditional 2-on-2, with our oldest acting as cornerback and his younger brother playing defensive tackle, up against a non-existent offensive line.

To be fair – our league values sportsmanship (when convenient) – when I am on offense, I will ask if the kids are ready before "snapping" the ball. One time, Youngest, playing DT, was pulling up grass when I asked if he was ready. "Yes," he eagerly replied. So, with my wife occupying Oldest, I just picked up the ball and ran. Even though my days as a dual-threat quarterback are behind me, I gained a good chunk of yards.

Sportsmanship, smortsmanship.

It was cute as hell though, and he has never made the same mistake again.

The Calling of the Plays

The play-calling situation in the DBMFL is also unique, since we do not have head coaches, offensive coordinators, or even the people that run onto the field with water bottles during time outs (yet). For the boys, it is very egalitarian: the three of us take turns making up plays and rotate which play gets called.

Youngest is hilarious. Since he wears a mouth guard that was originally designed for a Great White shark and refuses to take it out to call the play, Oldest and I get a spray of spittle and some gurgling sounds. Sometimes he will point. At least two times he actually pointed in the direction of the end zone. Nonetheless, when Youngest feels that he has effectively communicated his strategy, he'll slobber out "1-2-3!" and clap his hands. Off we go, and many times the "play" is successful.

Perhaps this is something that the NFL will borrow from us when they hit training camp to get ready for their regular season. The ol' gurgle'n'go offense.

Just like the grass-picking thing, if you cannot smile watching him do this, you have some sort of bacterial infection that has paralyzed the muscles in your face. See a doctor. Now.

For my wife and I, we just wing it, but not before drawing up the "play" in a manner in which the kids think they know what is coming. They have not quite figured it out, but anytime one yells "It is a run!" we pass. And vice versa.

Who Wins?

We do not keep score, and we do not have quarters or halves. The game ends when

180

someone starts to get pissed off and my wife or I call it to "end on a good note". If you are a parent, you know what I mean.

The vast majority of the time, everything goes great – the boys even take turns spiking the ball when they score. Two spikes for one touchdown is probably an unsportsmanlike conduct penalty in the NFL, but we tend to look the other way. The only celebration-related penalties we call are for dangerous play if the touchdown calls for a leaping chest bump and there is no pre-leap coordination. There have been a few close calls that made me happy that the kids were wearing mouthguards. But…tired, hungry, thirsty…we all have our limits, especially when there are perceptions of a missed coverage assignment.

Postseason?

We've yet to work out the play-off format since the DBMFL only has 1.5 teams. The league execs are pressuring us to have a Super Bowl regardless. If we can get a fraction of a fraction of a fraction of the ads revenue that the NFL enjoys, the DBMFL will be financially in the black for a generation. Since we play in summer, we are looking at "The DBMFL Super Bowl Halftime Show, brought to you by Li'l Jimmy's Lemonade stand." I can say this, however, regarding end of the season awards:

Oldest is offensive and defensive player of the year so far.

Youngest is the best DT and running back of the year.

I'm on track to be MVP (I am the only actual QB in the league – I kind of have to win, per Federal Law)

My wife is…uhm…leading the league in tackling and getting tackled.

With any luck, we will continue to grow and, in time, dupe the Howard County government into giving us a publicly funded stadium. In the end, that is always the main goal of a professional sports franchise.

Street Hockey Part 2

Two weeks after our first family foray into street hockey, I had recovered enough to give it another attempt. The family went back up to the flat parking lot again yesterday for some more hockey. (Flatness, in terms of kids on skates, and a street hockey ball, is critical. Both elements tend to abide by Newtonian Laws of Motion.) We had spent the last few days running around like crazy people, nursing butt pain (well, I was anyway) and tossing oblong balls at each other, in the vainglorious hope of making significant progress in terms of earned real

estate. Since the kids' mouth guards needed a
nice break, and the yard had reverted back to
"mud pit" status, we decided to change things up
once again.

Of course, the "family", in terms of
skating, meant just the boys, The reasons for
which have already been discussed.

We sat in the shade, on a soft batch of
grass next to a tree on one of the parking lot
islands. The kids were remarkably well-
disciplined with their hockey sticks. Sticks in
general, but certainly hockey sticks, are well-
documented implements of clubbing. We could
not believe that the kids were able to walk to the
lot and begin play without giving each other
multiple contusions. Sure, we do our best to
police activity. But these kids are clever, and the
desire to club that which ought not be clubbed is
strong. Sometimes, a clubbing or two slips
through the cracks. There is nothing nefarious
about clubbing – it is human nature. Give a
college kid a box of fireworks. Count the number
of fireworks and the number of fingers and toes.
Come back in four hours and see if the numbers
are all still the same. See what I mean?

The point is that the boys enjoyed skating
around the lot together, without any parental
assistance. After a few laps around the lot, they
would call for me to play hockey with them. For

183

a 2-on-1 situation, I think I fared rather well. I felt better, too. The last time, I could not properly enjoy scoring on the kids. This time, my pumped fist and high-five to myself told any onlookers that I was back to my old self.

In between my shifts on the "ice", our thoughts - (of the four of us) were all over the map.

Wife: "How far is it to the ER? And which of the males here is most likely to need to go there?"

Kid 1: "Chicken tenders for dinner again tonight?"

Kid 2: "I was thinking about a nice quiche."

Both kids: "AAAAAHAHAHAHAHA!

Me: "Why does my rump still hurt?"

Smoldering butt pain aside, it was really nice to just sit and relax. The boys were not doing anything horribly dangerous. Nonetheless, knowing that they could handle their self-preservation duties without mom and dad was a positive addition to the afternoon.

Then, with nirvana nearly achieved, we would go back to whipping nasty wrist shots at each other. A wrist shot – and this has been proven by science – is always crisper after meditation.

Rollerblades On/Rollerblades Off...Just pick already!

(There's a Bill Nye joke in there somewhere – "safety glasses on, safety glasses off".)

This time of relaxation, however, did not come without cost. Our youngest was rather insistent on consistently addressing his skate situation, removing, and putting back on, the skates as the situation dictated. At least "as the situation dictated in his mind" – there was nothing different from one moment to the next. He just wanted to change things up. If you are a parent, you know the fickleness of a 5-year-old regarding footwear.

Oldest was, more or less, fine with his foot situation, requiring only a few changes, mostly to shore up the level of ankle support. I suspect that most of his concern regarding the structural integrity of his skates/ankles was related to the previous experience of Dad falling on his rump and writhing around in a considerable amount of pain.

Foot-equipment issues aside, that we were in... I am not sure if a parking lot in suburban Maryland counts as "nature", but we were in it. The boys had fun thinking about eating chicken tenders yet again. My wife had fun wondering about emergency medical services and Google-mapping every possible route to the hospital. I had fun thinking...

...ouch.

Youth Sports

Before rec sports shut down, and hopefully when they return, every new season leads to a fun family ritual: the song, dance, and debate of selecting the recreational sport that our kids would like to participate in for the upcoming season. Now that things seemed to have eased (although all that can change tomorrow) it is time to rekindle that flame. While the boys do have a fondness for their Xbox1, they also enjoy getting out and about. And mom and dad will not let them rely on video games/technology for recreational activity. "Activity" is in the title; therefore, they have to be "active". Howard County does us a favor and belches out a recreational activity catalogue once a quarter or so, weeks in advance of the next season. This tome frequently exceeds 100 pages of exceptionally fine print.

While I very sincerely appreciate all of the options, I think that the county could spare a few editors so we can pare this back a bit. For starters, "Archery for 4-5-Year-olds" can't be all that much different than "Archery for 4–5-Year-olds Who Don't Like Salmon". We do not need a

My Vacuum Sucks

three-page entry for each. Also, while it is absolutely accurate, we can probably just generalize the parents' caveat up front, and not repeat it in each course description. Just state that your kids will learn an activity, and semi-qualified instructors will make sure that no one gets maimed. Instead, this is what we get:

"In Intro to Badminton, your child will learn introductory badminton skills such as serving, lobbing and resisting the urge to whack the snot out of other kids with a racket. Parents will have the opportunity to bury their faces in their phones, and text friends/family with stuff like 'Can you believe every other parent here is surgically welded to their phone?!' Participants will get a t-shirt."

I am, however, particularly fond of the standard weather statement that they include upfront, practically on the cover:

"In case of even the hint of inclement weather, be sure to dial the Weather Hotline at 410-xxx-xxxx once every five minutes to see if <activity> got cancelled and you can stay home, which we know you'd prefer after a rough day and a lousy commute."

With the vivid course descriptions out of the way, and the number of the Weather Hotline

187

etched into the memories of every parent, it was time to make some decisions.

Picking an activity

Over the years, we have learned to not toss the activity tome in the general direction of the kids and say, "Go nuts, guys." Inevitably, they would pick something like Contemporary Axe Throwing, which meets every Wednesday from 6-9 AM at the Howard County Axe Throwing Center, which is 45 minutes from our house. Hard no, for a lot of reasons, and lots of fussing.

"You're a terrible dad. All my friends know how to chuck a 17" blade into the skull of someone from 25 yards out!"

So, we carefully weed out the sports/locations/times that are simply too much of a pain-in-the-rear. As far as the kids know, that whole big book only contains three options that fit our schedule. It is like magic! Then, even with only three choices, we engage in a lengthy negotiating session that would make Senate Leader Mitch McConnell soil himself.

My oldest: "Point of procedural order: Intermediate Buccaneering is only 4.7 miles away from Basic Sitting, and at the exact same time."

Me: "Point of Order: Quiet you."

Eventually, agreements are made, sacrifices conceded, and a pact is formed. Dues are paid, and we receive a confirmation email once again emphasizing the free t-shirt.

Maintaining interest

One of the downsides to living in a county with so many people who want to do so many things, is that parents need to register their kids months in advance of the start of the activity. When the time rolls around, kids who are nine and five tend to forget after several weeks that they actually decided to do this activity.

Me: "Hey bud, ready for your first jousting class? I bet you are going to be awesome."

My oldest: "I don't want to go."

"But...that's what you chose...remember? You wanted to ride the horse?"

"I don't want to go."

"Well...this is the bed you made, time to lay in it."

"How is it that you are 40, I am nine, and yet your grasp of the English language is so poor: I. Do not. Want. To. Go."

Me: <calls Weather Hotline>

Mom: "Hey Slugger, ready for baseball?"

My youngest: "Mom, baseball is a girl's sport."

"Well, that really doesn't matter, but your league is all boys. That is why Daddy was out until 10PM last night trying to find a ShockObliterator 9000 Athletic Protector."

"There could be girls."

"There aren't."

"But there could be."

Mom: <calls Weather Hotline>

The games – or recreational activities – that we play.

Home Improvement, Snake Removal, and Incompetence

"Nor let us try the Lord, as some of them did, and were destroyed by the serpents."

- 1 Corinthians 10:9

When it comes to home improvement/household projects, I am what is known as a "12%er". I only ever actually finish 12 percent of the project. Typically, this means I will dream up some project that would take a seasoned professional several months to complete. I will gather some tools (or worse, buy new ones to replace those that I cannot find) and tackle steps 1-3 of Phase I. Then, right when the progress meter tips over the 12% mark, I take a break that I never return from.

To sate my primal need to tinker with stuff around the house, I have learned to stick to very basic tasks that can be completed before I feel the need to take a break. For example, I am quite fond of moving furniture. On the surface, it does not seem like that big a deal. But if you look carefully, you can see that the couch is facing a slightly different direction. And, after some necessary cleaning, I discovered that the pile of kids toys in the corner was just the armchair I have been looking for. It was simply too covered in crap that the kids never play with anymore.

I did actually complete a project once. It almost killed me. On a white-hot day – into triple digits – I decided to move ~50 heavy garden stones from the front yard to the backyard. Then, I covered the land that they were now bordering with mulch. I sweated so much that vast pools formed underneath me anytime I stood still. The "water" was so salty that even the Dead Sea was jealous. Neighborhood kids came from blocks away to float in the briny lakes. (Of course, their newfound buoyancy was short-lived: as soon as they got back to the community pool, they all sank like rocks tied to larger rocks. But I digress.)

But before I devolved into the kind of man that Father's Day cards make fun of, I was faced with a task that I needed to successfully complete. It was the first winter in our house, and failure was simply not an option.

The fauna of the mid-Atlantic

We live in suburban Maryland, which means we have three phyla of animals that naturally occur here: animals that damage your vehicle if you hit them, animals that are mere bumps in the road, and an insidious lot of animals that aim to take revenge on humans for killing Puffy the Slow-footed Squirrel – animals like mosquitoes and snakes.

I do not like snakes. To be clear, I do not have any bias against oddly elongated animals based solely on their body structure. There is no animus between the moray eel and I. Eels stay in water, and all I must do to avoid them is stay out of the water. Snakes though…those rapscallions are land based, and they can sneak into places. Like houses.

Ours is a split-level home nestled in one of those planned communities that popped up in the 1970s. On our street of 25 or so homes, there are three different floor plans. When you get through the front door of our brand of more "traditional" split-level, and into the foyer, you can go up a few stairs to our main living area or downstairs to a more austere level with a family room. Like any good family room on the lower level of a split-level home built in the 1970s, it has a nice fireplace and…a drop ceiling. There is also a half-bath that has seen its fair share of plumbing nightmares, since the toilet is less-than-capable of handling robust "action."

The drop ceiling is a solid three feet below the flooring above it and has the standard light fixtures with the translucent plastic tiles that allow light to enter the living space. The fixtures nestle between the upper-level flooring and the ceiling of the lower level. The whole set-up allows for a crawl space that is just tall enough to accommodate a toddler on all fours.

During the early days, the downstairs family room was the warmest of the rooms that could support a TV hooked up to cable. So, we spent most of those winter nights down there watching whatever was on that night, playing a game or two, or just sitting and talking about all of the wonderful home improvement plans I had for when the weather got warmer. As of this writing in 2021, none of those plans has advanced out of the "planning" phase. (Every piece of furniture we own, however, has been moved multiple times.) We had two cats at the time (we still have two cats, just different ones. The cats in this story are dead from old age), and they became increasingly agitated when in the family room – they enjoyed all of the blankets we had down there, but some unearthly presence was disturbing their bliss. At first, we thought they were just being dim because, if we are being honest, they were dim.

The dimmest actually ended up being the brightest, as fate would have it, and it would come to pass that he was right to be afraid.

Enter the serpent

One night after a fine dinner that relied heavily on our microwave, the dimmer of the bunch, Orion, was especially upset and stared at the ceiling. After a few seconds of thought, he let out a guttural "raaaaaawr." Additional investigation seemed prudent. Since whatever college basketball game was on was not holding my attention, I had the time to poke around.

I retrieved a five-iron whose shaft had become bent during one of the (many) times I moved my golf clubs from one place to another in the house. (Playing golf is a lot like home improvement for me: I say I am going to do it; I have the tools and the means to do so, I just...do not.) I used my bent rod to tap the ceiling, fully expecting to hear the pitter-patter of mice feet as they scurried to safer locales.

Nope.

Instead, we heard a sound similar to what you hear when you slowly drag your hand over your sofa cushion — a patient slithering noise. Looking at one of the clear light-bearing tiles that was directly over our heads, we saw a serpent that had clearly been sent to scout for good real estate for a new gateway to hell.

"Coming soon! The Shops at Chrestfield! Featuring Bill's Barber and Body Piercing, the Dollar Tree, Hank's Ethiopian Market and a brand-new Gateway to Hell!"

A cautious inquiry into the ceiling space confirmed the worst. Cue Samuel L. Jackson's voice making a profane proclamation about the location of a snake. The snake was roughly .42 miles long and as thick as a Honda Pilot. It had clearly recently consumed several large African cats the origins of which continue to befuddle me to this day.

Panic. And not the slow panic that envelops the heroes of *Jurassic Park 18: Shouldn't We be in a Different Era by Now?* when they realize that the velociraptors have learned how to turn invisible. This was instant panic. Please recall that I am not fond of this brand of animal. I do not wish them any particular ill will. I just don't want to be anywhere near them, and now at least one is *living in my house.*

A hastened review of the structural layout of the space confirmed that the leviathan snake was confined to that part of the house — it could not, absent any sort of fire-breathing abilities that could scorch a hole in the wafer-thin walls of our house, access other areas in our home (which, at this point, still seemed to be in play).

Immediately, we closed off the room and called the first government agency I could think of. The public library system wondered why I had called them about this but were very polite in telling me to seek help elsewhere. I also added to my arsenal:

1) My slightly bent (and unused for golf) five iron was employed for long-range justice. I figured that it would be effective from 3' to 6'.

2) An unused handyman's hammer —
claw-side out — was deployed for short-range
justice. If this beast got within 3', I figured that
panicked swinging could erase the threat. I'm
glad I didn't have a gun – only God and an
engineer from the 70's knew how much
structural damage I could have caused if this
thing escaped and got uppity.

Armed for defense (think Desert Shield
in 1990-91) we called a pest-control company for
advice. The best they could offer was:

*"Just throw up some glue boards and wait for
the snake to a) leave or b) get stuck and see what
happens."*

See what happens? What the hell does
that mean? How – precisely – do snakes respond
to getting stuck to stuff? Do they gain an ability
to spit venom-laced fangs at you? Perhaps their
fellow gang members kidnap prominent
Hollywood stars? Shouldn't you have some basic
idea of how this is going to play out?

He added:

*"You can pay us $100 to do it or spend $7.99
and do it yourself".*

So, that is what we did (the $7.99
option), but with extreme caution. Glue boards
and patience. I unwrapped the glue boards,

yelled "fire in the hole!" and tossed it on into the ceiling. After the first few days of popping my head into the ceiling to see if the snake had been snagged, I had abandoned my golf club — the space constrictions made it ineffective in times of crisis — and only brought my hammer with me for such ventures. If any justice needed to be meted out, it would be a close-combat type. Here, the library was quite helpful. They have a curiously large array of titles that focus on Navy SEAL hand-to-hand combat training.

The plan takes shape

Finally, we had success. During my usual check on the herpetological stand-off in the lower level of my house, I discovered a snake, who was probably a little upset, stuck to the plastic board. It was go time. As the exterminator said on the phone, time to "see what happens."

My wife was still at work, so I had a glass of Jim Beam whiskey and plotted my next moves.

Step 1: Have a glass of Maker's Mark whiskey

Step 2: Call wife to implore her to arrive ASAP (even though she really had no need or desire to dawdle on her way home)

Step 3: Have wife handle snake situation, and
release it back into the wild hundreds of yards
from our house

The idea was to carefully remove the
ceiling tiles to inch just close enough to the
snake/board combination to hook the snake out
of the ceiling and into a large trash can we
placed on the floor. I figured that this would not
be too traumatic for the snake. Luckily, the cats
wanted no part of the goings-ons and were not a
hindrance. I have seen TV shows – this is not a
joke – where a snake will try to jump from one
tree to another, miss, land on the ground, and
slither away seemingly unharmed.

The plan worked. Within a few minutes
we were hauling a snake-filled trashcan down to
a pond that once served as a water source for an
old orchard (I have no idea what the neighbors
thought when they saw us walking about the
neighborhood with a trash can during the day).
The orchard itself had long since been plowed
under so houses like mine could be built.
Perhaps that furthered the snake's displeasure
with us. Was our house built on his/her ancestral
homeland? Who knows? All that matters is that
we were able to release the snake from the glue
board and back into snake civilization. As much
as I do not like the things, I do not want to kill
them.

I assume that the snake went into hibernation since it was still late winter. There must have been a mighty raucous party that spring.

"Hey guys, Lumpy is back! C'mere you! Tell us all about what you've been up to!"

We still had to figure out how the snakes were outsmarting us

It turns out that Lumpy was not our first guest. We found several snake skins up in the ceiling that were too big for Lumpy, unless s/he had some degenerative spine disorder that caused him/her to shrink. Lumpy also would not be the last. There were at least two other snakes that made our home theirs in the post-Lumpy era before I found out how they were getting into our abode. There was a hole where the chimney met the foundation that was just big enough for a snake of modest carriage. You can rest assured that I immediately acquired, and applied, enough industrial grade sealant to keep out single-celled organisms. It was so tight that the Chernobyl Radiation Containment Unit sent over a team to author a report.

They were nice people and did not like snakes. Just for fun, I Googled "snakes native to Ukraine." I do not think that I would like it there: they have two kinds of venomous vipers tooling around their steppes. Goodness only knows what effect all that nuclear waste had on the local vipera ursini population...

Fitness Part III - Burning Calories as a Family in Nature

"Between every two pines there is a doorway to a new world." - John Muir

We took the kids to a national park to go hiking a few weekends ago. There are not a lot of good hiking weekends in the summer around here (I guess if the heat in Arizona is referred to as a "dry heat", our summers have a "wet heat"). There is – allegedly – a nice waterfall near us so we figured to give it a go, even though waterfalls in Central Maryland are mostly disappointments. They are small trickles of water that succumb to gravity when they get to the edge of a 10-foot "cliff". And that is if you are lucky, and it has recently rained. It had not recently rained. Still, there are tons of fun/unexpected things to see out in nature. For example, while on the trail this time we met Danish people (people actually from Denmark and not dessert bakers). At about this time, our kids were marveling at a black snake that was slithering along the trunk of a fallen tree. While I don't like snakes, and certainly not if they try to sneak into my house, the kids are unperturbed by their presence. The Danes were aghast that we would allow our children to get so close to such an evil serpent, and immediately thought to have local authorities quarantine the area. My wife pointed out that the snake was no more dangerous than any of the trees in the forest. I think they still thought we were terrible parents. And that was just one unrelated anecdote that helped to offset the eventual disappointment of the falling water.

But back to the beginning...

The drive

Like any good park, Catoctin Mountain Park is located at least an hour from our house, this time, in Frederick County. For context, locals refer to the county as "F-Red-Neck County. Like any good suburban family, we over-packed in order to exist in nature for more than two hours. Thank goodness we had our hybrid minivan to efficiently get us to the park and to store enough supplies to sustain a lengthy stay in some desolate land in Central Asia. We had more water on board than the Gobi Desert sees in three decades (and, ironically, more water than went over the "falls" in an hour). Our non-perishable snack roster was robust. My wife and I even quibbled over whether or not to pack crossbows.

Me: "Are you sure that we need two crossbows?"

Wife: "Bears."

Me: "Fair point, but there will be a lot of people on the trail that are slower than us. Plus, I don't know where my crossbow license is."

We set off from one part of suburban Maryland to another part of suburban Maryland that had more trees and a neat waterfall. Even though Frederick County is only two counties over (Carroll County gets in the way for about four miles) it is a different world over there in some ways. The main gas stations are a different brand, and they still have more than one International House of Pancakes per town.

After the standard progression of major highway to medium road to tiny road with lots of superfluous turns, we were "lucky" enough to park about 1/3 of a mile away from the park entrance. Forget actually parking in the park. Like I mentioned, nice hiking days are rare, and waterfalls are few and far between. The Park is also home to Hog Rock. (Seriously – apparently there was a time when we let acne-laced middle schoolers name geological features), which attracts the local stoner crowd.

The hike

The Appalachian Mountains are nature's A-cups. They are merely lumps in the land. They would not need the extra support of a sports bra if they went for a jog, their majesty eroded away over billions of years of not growing like the far more impressive Rockies or Alps. Still, for an old man like me, even the slightest change in elevation is onerous. As of this writing, my knees, ankles, and spleen are still sore and at least three such elements need surgical replacement. The hike went well, however. It was a nice 4-ish mile walk through trees with multi-colored leaves with minimal damage from invasive insects, nice views of the road below, lined on either side by Lexuses, BMWs, hybrid vans, etc., and Danish people who were unnecessarily scared of impotent snakes (I checked: there are only two species of snakes in Denmark).

The only problem, however, came when we would encounter other people on the trail. At 15 yards out, some preternatural voice would yell out to all the parties involved: "FIRE IN THE HOLE!". Naturally, everyone would dive off to the side of the one lane path opening it up for passage for whoever was brave enough to remain standing. This introduced a whole other host of health issues. For one, mountains have lots of rocks. Haphazardly flying into the wilderness could result in massive head wounds, broken ribs, or a nasty tennis elbow. You could also land next to a gang of snakes that were pretty pissed off at the xenophobic Danes, and looking for revenge against any human, regardless of their nationality.

We pressed on and, after all the sprained ankles, we made it to the majestic waterfall. Something seemed off. Where was all the water that was supposed to be falling? A quick check of one of the phones in my pocket (I was waiting to see if anyone replied to a comment on a cable news website's article) confirmed the worst: it had not rained in days. The "falls" appeared as nothing more than a large man with prostate issues constantly urinating on a rock. So, back we went. During the return trip, the kids were noticeably (and understandably) disappointed. I resisted the urge to fan the flames with something like: "that's what you get for taking such a long shower – you used all the water!"

The aftermath

After walking two miles to see what it would look like if a giant had flow issues, we walked two more miles back to the car. Given the parking situation, even when we finished the trail part we were still in danger. Tired, sore, and saddened over the leaky faucet we spent all day getting to, we still had to navigate a considerable stretch of mountain road devoid of a shoulder. When the budget allows, the Maryland State Department of Resources should figure out a way to increase the parking occupancy for an enormous park. Seven narrow parking spots is way too few. Here's a tip: pave over that lousy waterfall. I have never been to Hog Rock, but it must be a better attraction.

Unlike most squirrels in Maryland, our family was able to cross the road and safely access the vehicle. A quick check of our supplies showed that we still had enough sustenance to last 28 more days if needed.

We were safely ensconced in our suburbanite vehicle. On the way back, hours after our usual lunchtime, we decided to pick up some authentic Mexican food to soften the sounds of growling stomachs (but later deal with the Rage o' the Bowels). From Qdoba.

Time to replenish those calories

Nature had taken its toll on us, both emotionally and physically. We absolutely needed to get nourishment as soon as humanly possible. Luckily, we are a technically savvy family. We were able to use a combination of the van and one of our phones to locate a convenient Q, peruse the authentic menu, and call-in our order. That meant that, upon arrival, my wife could just hop out, cross the lot, and retrieve our authentic lunch. Once back inside the comfort of the climate-controlled van (the prohibition on eating in the van had long been gone – with two kids, we knew it would never last) with our food, we got to eliminating nature from our systems and replacing it with food from a lab.

All seemed to go well. The order was correct, the temperature of the food indicated that most bacteria had been killed, and according to the GPS we were only 18 minutes away from our destination (home). However, once we got home disaster struck. My wife could not find her phone and a thorough family-wide search yielded nothing. She called the Qdoba and <whew> they had it.

So that was the coda to our family nature hike/exercise outing: my wife – sweaty, dirty, tired, and sore – heading back to Qdoba to retrieve the phone that we used to order carry-out authentic "casual fast" Mexican food.

We are lucky to also live close to nature

We actually do not have to travel any real distance to get to nature. Just a short walk from our house, we can walk past a few ponds and then access a trail system that goes for 20+ miles or so. Admittedly, the backbone of the nature trail system is a drainage stream that collects rainwater run-off from hundreds (if not thousands) of development projects. Just across from the "stream" at the point we access the trails there are two gas stations, a Jiffy Lube and a full auto repair shop. The back end of the property abuts a steep hill that flows downward into, you guessed it, the stream. No one has any idea what is in that water, but it can melt a pair of Crocs in five seconds. We do, however, know what else is on that hill: rusted out laundry machines, a few bed frames and a burned-out car that might have been used in a mob hit in the 1980s. Luckily, nature has re-taken over some of what humans have taken from it. If you can ignore the broken beer bottles, it is really pretty nice.

We had to take an injury time out for a few weeks after our sojourn to Frederick County but got back in the proverbial saddle last night.

We started out down the 200-yard stretch of sidewalk to get to the ponds. We recently learned that the ponds by our house were originally created to be a water source for an apple orchard. The orchard would later close shop because it relied on labor from high schoolers and paid them roughly 24.5 cents an hour. When the high schoolers started to realize that they could make $7 + tips at Starbucks, the orchard lost its labor force. As soon as this happened, developers moved in and replaced the rows of fruit bearing trees with houses that are too big for the land on which they are built.

My youngest did his thing. He likes to lag behind a bit so he can skip past Mom and Dad to rejoin his brother at the head of the column. Eventually, once Skippy caught up, we all made it to the trail that leads to the ponds, for once without any scraped knees or sore feelings.

"Dad! He threw something at me!"

"Was it a poisonous snake?"

"No..."

"Then just keep going."

The boys have not been very observant on our more recent nature walks. This is not necessarily their fault – the circuit is, more or less, the same thing every time. Still, this is – obviously – rather antithetical to my philosophy of constant observation and appreciation. I showed them some music videos for songs that struck this chord for me (and interspersed those songs with some Metallica and Megadeth to keep them awake). The idea was to inspire imagination and observation. It seemed to work. Either that, or it inspired them to fake it to get me off their back. I also gave them each a black Sharpie.

From my previous life, I have a ton of white t-shirts. For every collared white button-down shirt, there are at least two white t-shirts with sagging necklines and grotesque pit stains. Some of these tees are in a state of disrepair. By "disrepair" I mean "massive holes in the armpit region". These shirts only offered protection if I spontaneously began lactating. (Even then, milk is white.)

I threw on an anti-man-milk t-shirt and told the boys to use the markers to write anything they did not expect to see on my shirt.

We saw lots of neat things. There was a beautiful blue jay devouring seeds. The cynic inside of me thought that was a strange form of infanticide. But I did not let that ooze out. We glimpsed a momma robin feeding her babies. There was a painted turtle that was the size of a trash can lid. All of these things made it onto my decrepit white t-shirt. They had expected to see a turtle, but not one that large. This thing was the "Andre the Giant" of pond turtles. Our family was even lucky enough to peep in on a heron stalking a fish in the shallows. As we watched, the heron struck, and plucked a fish out of the water. We saw it navigate the fish into its mouth and looked on as the doomed ἰχθύς flopped its way down the bird's throat and into its belly, the outline of the fish visible as it made its descent.

Luckily, the boys refrained from writing some of the less-savory elements of the evening. Some examples of (thankfully) undocumented observations:

1 – Youngest peeing in the woods. It took a good bit of strategizing to make sure that he was out of the sight of other nature lovers. Discretion is especially crucial because he likes to turn around a few seconds early. While surreptitious outdoor

whizzing is, in fact, a feat worth noting, I am happy that it did not make it onto my shirt (it is also not unexpected).

2 – Goose poop. We observed a lot of goose poop. So much so that even a young fawn with tiny hooves could not negotiate the trail without having pounds of goose poop permanently affixed to its hooves. Just like the turtle, the presence was expected, just not the size/amount.

3 – Fishermen. We saw five "outdoorsmen" who took to the ponds in the fading daylight to try and wrangle a 3"- 4" fish from the water. These are manufactured ponds that are ringed by houses that go for $300-400k. If you need/want to fish to relax, go nuts. But you probably do not need a tackle box that can hold enough gear to boat 18+ yellow fin tuna and/or tiger sharks. Most of the rugged gentlemen had camouflage "trucker" style hats to make sure that the fish could not see them.

4 – Unkept Yards. There is a yard on our circuit that has not been mowed since – best I can figure – 1976. It is magnificent to see the long stalks of grass that have been bred by Home Depot to grow in dense shade, sway in the breeze. It would just be less out of place if it were not bordered by two really well-tended yards. Also, there is significant circumstantial evidence – a dramatic increase in gnu carcasses, for example

– that a pride of lions has settled onto the property.

All of the silly stuff aside, we did see a lot of neat nature-y things thriving in the fabricated hellscapes of suburbia. My holey t-shirt now reflects that. When we go for another walk, I will toss it back on, armpits free to breathe, and hand out more Sharpies.

In one walk alone, we have seen lots of cool things. Birds feeding their babies regurgitated worms, birds crapping all over public walkways, birds eating fish whole, and birds (geese) getting pissed off at other birds (geese) and trying to fight them.

Turns out, birds are assholes. If one of the kids wanted to add that to a shirt, I would oppose them.

All that said, the boys are learning to be more observant, we get out and get active as a family, and they record our observations.

Also, most importantly, if bare armpits can absorb Vitamin D, my daily intake is robust even while wearing a shirt.

The Sugar Wars

"When diet is wrong, medicine is of no use. When diet is correct, medicine is of no need." - Ayurvedic Proverb

Sugar. If there is a more addictive collection of white granules, I'd love to hear about it. From Skittles to Milk Duds (y'all are selling yourselves short: there is nothing dud-y about them. In fact, they should be called "Milk: Finally, a Useful Application), I love all things candy. I mentally refer to the cats as Sugar1 and Sugar2, even though I use their Christian names - Moo and Dumbledore - when addressing them aloud. I even love the Spanish word for sugar: azucar. It sounds like a bad-ass warrior mage with one of those outlandishly large swords who loves to terrorize Hobbit towns.

"Oh raspberries", said Thom Furgood, "it looks like the Azucar is back. I just know he'll wreck my turnip crops again..."

"And kill 40% of the town's population," replied Oliver Shavenrump.

"Right, that too...pity."

When you start measuring your intake in "mega-grams" instead of "grams", you go from the whimsical Candyland to the dourer Land of the Damned, where high blood pressure and death lurk behind every lollipop ladder.

How can one replace pure, uncut, sugar?

As I have aged, I have felt more and more of a push to start seeing a doctor. That push's name is Leah. I married her in 2008 and she started to become concerned when a harem

217

of happy hummingbirds started following me and making increasingly bold attempts to get at my sweet nectar (read: blood with 35% SBV – sucrose by volume). After one especially sobering doctor appointment, the orders were crystal clear: find a way to significantly cut back, or eliminate, unhealthy sugars. My wife is the family health nut. She knows that a regular apple is better for the pancreas than a candied apple. Thanks to her, we know that corn, packed in a life-preserving serum and stored in an aluminum can has far more nutritional value than Candy Corn. (I must admit that the canned zombie corn also tasted better than its candy cousin.) Corn grows in the dirt. According to ancient alien astronaut theorists, Candy Corn grows in a large U.F.O. hovering over Antarctica.

Off she went - with two boxes of chocolate for "research" purposes - to the Modern Library of American Health: Google. We (she) eliminated aspartame right quick. Even though it took care of many of the sugar-centric issues, it brought a whole smorgasbord of side effects to the party. Spontaneous polydactyly for one. Another was a massive increase in the chance for inner ear tumors that ooze puss that smell like steamed broccoli. We all know that anything that smells healthy, but is not, is a trap. Even Hollywood routinely gets that part right.

Young archaeologist: "Doctor, this apse that was carved out of the cave wall and protected by fierce mummies smells...healthy. Like fresh chopped radishes."

Grizzled doctor/explorer: "Radishes? OUT! NOW!"

"But Doctor Skullhunter, we are so close!"

"I said get out dammit!" <spits on cave floor, is killed by spears made of Legos>

A solution! (maybe)

Just when the beacon of hope was all-but-extinguished, there came an answer: sugar alcohol. Could it be? The replacement is far superior to that which was to be replaced? I am well north of 21, so getting rum-infused Rolos would be no issue at all! Well, you know what they say: if it appears to be too good to be true, you're either the lucky .000000000000001% or a gullible dingus.

It turns out it was not *that* kind of alcohol. Look, science: The English language has hundreds of thousands of words. Hell, we even steal words from other languages.

"Sorry, Billy: sake, enchilada, and Big Mac aren't English words."

Just pick another less confusing/promising word. Still, it seemed like a good compromise. It was not the bad kind of sugar, but it was not the good kind of alcohol either. It did not have any obvious side effects and most major candy companies had sugar alcohol versions of their more popular lines. You will never see me eating off-brand candy like a Gelatinous Thorax bean or a Happy Herdsman hard candy. Off we went to the Modern American Everything Market (Amazon) to make our (my) selections and feverishly click "refresh" on the Track Package page.

"Your method of escape from the Dungeon of Diabetes is 8 stops away. Look! Here is a helpful map to prove it!"

Upon arrival, it was glorious. Before me lay a regal spread of soft beans all the colors of the rainbow and a fine spread of hard sugar logs. I have always gorged on new things (when I bought a new 89" UltraMega18.8kHDTV, I found myself up at 3:30AM watching a 2-hour infomercial for a super sealant/ adhesive glue/ military grade explosive – the detail was exquisite). In less than 15 minutes, I had taken down close to 30 servings of this stuff. Little did I know, this would be the last solid food I would see for quite some time.

The shadow side effect

Remember, in an earlier section of this remarkable piece of literature, when I referred to the children's board game "Candyland"? Well, this section is all about "Chutes and Ladders", with a heavy focus on the chutes. It started innocently enough, like the first offshore white cap in advance of a major hurricane. I am quite used to rumbles of gas that move about my abdominal cavity. Whereas some people have "ironclad" stomachs, my GI tract is made of balsa wood. Family car rides often devolve into spirited games of "Daddy or Open Landfill." For weeks after we purchased a new car my wife thought that a disgruntled dealership employee hid a dead fish in the spare tire well. Every time she brought it up, I just sheepishly replied "Uh...yes...smells like sea bass."

Likely, dinner was acting up and I would have to open some windows and turn up the TV. Within a few hours and a rushed trip to the can, I would be back to normal. Alas, things started to get worse. By the time the kids had gone to bed, the intensity of the gas pain had forced me to shift awkwardly while on the couch watching baseball. My wife looked at me with some concern, and not wanting to reveal the true cause of the discomfort, I produced a plausible alternative theory. "I think I pulled a muscle practicing – think fast – discus."

It was not long until the truth came out, if you know what I mean...

I will not belabor the point too much, but things were getting dodgy. The frequency of blasts of fetid air had increased to the point where one burst did not have enough time to fully dissipate before another came forth and added to the noxious mix. Within an inning of the baseball game, the air quality had degraded to the point where any living thing with the gift of self-propulsion had vacated the room.

Still, I was feeling good. Dieting is all about feeling good about oneself, and I felt rather good about having the couch all to myself.

The torrent that came with Phase II hit a few hours later, presaged by an unholy guttural noise that lasted 22 minutes. That was followed by the sound of my feet smacking onto the hardwood floor, loudly tracing my trip through the house en route to the bathroom. It was time for "Chutes and Ladders". Luckily, there were not any ladders involved - the GPS system in whatever had grown in my duodenum preferred southerly routes.

In a calm British female voice: "Continue south on present route for the next 6 hours."

As the sun made its way up and over the Eastern horizon, I was a broken man who felt as though he had played 5 consecutive football games as an undersized defensive lineman. I prayed that one final convulsion would wretch my soul from my now severely dehydrated body and release my Earthly presence from its state of agony. Shortly thereafter, however, I was able to wobble back to bed. (As Pliny the Elder wrote in his historical account of the Sicilian Runs of 45A.D., "forsooth! There is no more poop to poop.") Under a hefty blanket, I spent the balance of the morning, and a few afternoon hours, convalescing.

When I emerged, well, that is when the fun started. I don't say that facetiously. It really was fun! With the lava chambers empty, the only thing coming down the shoot was the gassy aftermath. Even when the gas was not actively being expelled, more was forming as the seismic activity died down. The boys and I sat in silence waiting for the next outburst, as each had its own unique sounds and style. Would the next outpouring of gas be a short and sharp tweet? Or a long rumble that touched several octaves?

Afternoon turned to evening which in turn transitioned to night. The kids went to bed, followed by my wife. I brought up the rear. The last thing I remember thinking was "I sure hope to be able to handle solid foods sometime this month."

I woke up a few hours later than usual the next day feeling close to normal – I will call it 65% - and rejoined the family in the living area. On my way, I passed through the kitchen and noticed one of the empty bags that had previously held Hell's candy. There, in print that was so fine that an eagle-eyed falcon would have difficulty spotting them was a warning that read "this stuff makes Ex-Lax look like a placebo. Don't eat two bags in one sitting, dingus."

It was the second time in less than 24 hours that something had referred to me as a "dingus." Two yellow cards equal a red, so I was excluded from additional candy intake.

Civic Responsibility: My Brush with Activism

"It can be difficult to speak truth to power. Circumstances, however, have made doing so increasingly necessary." - Aberjhani

I woke up this morning determined to change the world. For the first time ever (that was not the result of a drunken dare), I called my elected officials to constructively complain about something. I like to fancy myself as being a responsible citizen who knows the key issues affecting the country, my state, and my local district.

I am aware that my state has a bicameral legislature, and I vote in most elections. Especially if Mr. T is on the ballot. Even if he is not, I write him in when I feel like it. If I am the only one in my county who votes in the race for Commissioner of Public Library Fines, guess who wins.

Commissioner T, fool. I can only imagine how that phone conversation goes. "Hello Mr. T, this is Gary Burkinson from the Howard County Board of Elections..."

I also try to keep up with the issues in order to make a serious and informed decision on the host of local ordinances that clutter up my ballot. Public works projects, budget issues...on all of these things I can step up to the voting booth and show you how to swing. But no man can know all, and I find myself punting on whether or not earthworms should be afforded privileged status under Medicare.

I spring into action

So, while I knew that I — theoretically — had delegates, I had no idea who they were or how to contact them. Luckily, Google — who had recently taught me that earthworms already have their own Federal health insurance program — would almost certainly have the answer. They did and were even able to give me some leads on how to obtain relevant contact information.

Holy hell. I had no idea how many districts we have in my state. Our house alone has three of them. This means that our cats, who spend hours a day washing themselves, have a delegate in our state's House of Delegates (the MD-3,410th District). Several websites helpfully offered to help me find my district and, by extension, my local officials. However, each one wanted me to "share my device's location." No way, man. I am not going to share my location with www.findyourcorporatetool.com.cn. Especially since the Washington Post recently wrote a multi-story epic on how easy it is to hack electronic devices.

Nonetheless, my dumb ass was able to persevere and figure out that my district was represented by multiple delegates and a state senator. Without divulging my location to Pakistani hackers, I was also able to use the tips Google gave me to obtain my representatives' contact information. The dawn of a new era of political action was nigh. Until it was not.

I make contact...kind of

I started calling at 10:01 EDT on a Monday. Crickets. Each office's line went to voicemail. There are several significant issues currently facing my state, and the nation. I would have thought that someone would have picked up the phone on a weekday at a time that was in-between most coffee breaks and lunch. Shouldn't there at least be someone in the office to check on the mousetraps in the staff lounge? Surely it could not have been an issue with phone bank staffing, unless their number is one digit off of a Chinese take-out joint. How many calls could they possibly get in one day?

I would even have settled for a high school intern who is making no money and risking a toxic interaction with a massively unhappy constituent just for a line on their resume that no one is going to ever care about.

"Hey, that's neat Jim — you wrote press releases about old people who managed to stagger their way to their 100th birthday. But this is a big-boy company. Here is a link to Arby's online job application. Coming up with a replacement for 'we have the meats' is probably more up your alley."

(That was actually a role I had when I interned at a local politician's office.)

Undeterred, but pissed off, I dutifully went about my civic duty. All of the voicemail greetings were delightfully generic and were read in a monotone that indicated an advanced level of soul-decay. I get a more vigorous automated response when I call the makers of Reynolds Wrap aluminum foil to complain about the sharpness of the teeth on the box.

Instead of multiple versions of:

"Thank you for calling the office of delegate <X>. If you leave your name, phone number, address, and whether you have an 'innie' or an 'outtie', we will get in touch with you."

I would greatly prefer a more honest approach:

"In a few minutes, when I am done with this patronizing introductory message, you will hear a beep. Leave a 10-15 second missive on whatever seems to be bothering you today. When the intern gets back from picking up my Viagra prescription, they will check it, laugh about your idealism, and get back to writing about the new squash court we funded for the senior center on Yucca Street."

Or, more likely:

"This is Doug Nutter, delegate of the MD-21st District and owner of Doug's HVAC. If you have a question or concern about the new bridge project over the Patapsco River, press 1. To contact me for an HVAC quote, press 2."

Democracy is tough

I somehow managed to get my message across without swearing — although I came close a few times. I engaged with my elected officials (or their proxies) after taking an inordinate amount of time trying to find out who the crap they were (and also potentially exposing my banking information to the Iranian Qods Force). I made an impassioned plea in furtherance of my cause (without divulging any information regarding the structural status of my belly button).

At least I can say I tried. Later in life, when my children ask about what it takes to be a good citizen, I will not be lying when I tell them that I have called my delegates and state Senators about an issue that was important to me. I'm sure they will follow up and ask what that issue was. I shall reply:

"I don't know – something about free HVAC stuff and bridges for earthworms. Kids, never underestimate the electoral power of the elderly, the gun lobby....and the earthworms."

I have to imagine that this is exactly what the framers of the U.S. Constitution had in mind when they reached back to the writings of intellectual giants like Hobbes, Locke, and Montesquieu to create a new government.

The Olympic Cycle: Witnessing Excellence

"The Olympics are a wonderful metaphor for world cooperation, the kind of international competition that's wholesome and healthy, an interplay between countries that represents the best in all of us."

- John Williams

It is time, once again, for the Olympics. Every two years (give or take - since the Winter Olympics are played in the winter, and the Summer Games predictably kick off in the summer) I will go in eyes wide open and enjoy all of the sport and spectacle.

Yes, I know that the whole franchise is built on commercialism and a slavish devotion to making money and exploiting human accomplishments. Nonetheless, I sincerely enjoy those accomplishments even if every aspect of the competition has an official sponsor.

Some make sense. Having Chuck's Lumber be the official lumber supplier of the Olympic hurdles kind of works. But Hello Kitty sponsoring the 10-meter diving platform is just confusing. Cats do not even like water. Such issues are easily surmountable, just like home improvement projects if you use Chuck's wood.

The sports that only make American TV during the Olympics

I love the sports that are novelties in the United States but are taken deadly seriously by other cultures, often leading to generations-long blood feuds. These sports that are rarely on American TV also make it easier for my wife and I to watch together, as she does not have to deal with me constantly citing old baseball players, events, and complaining about a team's relay throw strategy with less than two outs.

Badminton is one such sport. Here, badminton is a chance for middle-aged parents to waddle around a section of yard marked off by flimsy tape and whack a birdie at each other.

In Asia, badminton is life or death. It is a carefully played game of chess in which a shuttlecock is manipulated over several shots to earn a well-placed kill shot.

Commentator: "We all knew it would come down to this: Wang Dongfei and his sister Wang Zhuzhi versus the brother/sister combination of Dong Huze and Dong Leifeng. Right now, in center court, you can see the ceremonial bloodletting, which means we are almost ready. Coming up next live on MSCNBCSports, Wangs, Dongs and a cock. So much more than a gold medal at stake."

When my wife and I were in Jamaica for our honeymoon, a Jamaican sprinter – training for the Olympics - took us out on a catamaran. This is no joke: he knew at least 50 other sprinters competing for spots on the team. He knew their times, their splits, their strengths and weaknesses, how good their starts were, etc. It was insane. Even though it is a relatively small island, he had the entire sprinting scene dialed in

– even as he took two tourists out into the bay to look at a sunken cannon from a pirate ship.

The commentary

Over the years, NBC has, more or less, stuck with the tried-and-true strategy of having a general play-by-play guy in the booth who is paired up with an expert in the sport. The generalist gives us helpful information such as the name of the sport, the general point and who appears to be winning. The expert walks a fine line between conveying sport-specific information and way too much esoteric detail. Last night, the expert drifted into the latter during the single sculls preliminary heats, giving PhD level lectures on the science behind not tipping the boat.

It is a three-foot wide boat that weighs less than a toddler. I get it. We do not need this conversation to last several 7-minute heats.

I love when, nearing the end of the 8th heat of the 50km racewalk, the general guy finally breaks and says something like "Thanks Gary, I think we'll all remember that when we have to briskly walk 50km." And Gary, not getting the finer points of sarcasm launches right into a detailed explanation of what exactly starts happening to one's ankle ligaments at the 45th kilometer. The desperation of these folks to convey just how awesome their sport is can be made even more clear when you then watch the analysts for sports that more regularly cross the American sports radar. Those gymnastic types don't even bother to impress, whipping out all kinds of lingo that the average American is familiar with and understands.

The woebegone "also ran"

But the early heats are more than studies in the differences between the various weightlifting disciplines. They are displays of scintillatingly bad athletic performances. By the time the finals come around, all these dopes have long since been weeded out. Sure, the Andorran high jumper might be the best in his country, but on the international stage he crashed out after miraculously clearing 3 feet but stalling at 3'2". As Hank Hankerson pointed out in the cool, even cadence that he is known for in the international high jumping community, even a chihuahua can easily clear that.

In one real example we watched, a rower from Sudan was competing in a preliminary heat in a 2,000-meter race. She finished more than two minutes after the leaders. Since NBC was airing the race live, they cut to commercial after the top three automatic qualifiers finished and returned – this is not a joke – just in time to catch the Sudanese Steamboat stagger across the finish line.

I get it: chasing a dream, spirit of competition and whatnot. But a lot of these poor sods are doomed from the moment when they strap on their goggles...for a track event.

Pulling for Team USA

Those guys, the sods, are easy to root for, if for no other reason than you will not have to root for them for long. My relationship with rooting for American athletes has been more complicated. I know that seems sacrilegious since I am an American, but I started watching the Olympics in 1988 and am old enough to remember the Dream Team we sent over to Barcelona to compete in basketball. It did not really seem in line with the spirit of competition to use the world's most accomplished players to clobber some team from Hungary. That poor team had only seen a basketball for the first time a few weeks ago and managed to scrape together a few practices in between herding goats in the mountains outside of Debrecen.

Around that time American swimmers had huge advantages. Our A-Team was being outfitted with scientifically designed swimsuits that cost more than a Corvette. Eventually, these sharkskin megasuits were outlawed precisely due to the unfair competitive advantages they offered the wearer. Meanwhile, the team from Paraguay only kind of knew what a pool was and became flummoxed when the body of water did not have any fish in it.

I always rooted for the U.S. teams/competitors in less popular sports. I have always been all-in with Team USA handball, volleyball, and fencing. Even water polo to a certain extent. I hate getting splashed and having to tread water, two "skills" that are essential in this "sport".

Of course, the world has changed. Most athletes nowadays have access to the nutrition, training opportunities, and technology as their American counterparts. Many, if not most, athletes train in the United States. Except for the Swiss Surfing team. The Swiss Olympic Surfing Federation had been underfunded for decades. Maybe they will make it someday – it would be the first time a surfer competed in swimmies.

"His scheduled list of tricks consists entirely of 'not drowning'." "No nose side 740s?" "Nope. Just 'not drowning'."

So, until the International Olympic Committee introduces another sport that is quintessentially American and is dominated by the U.S.A. – like competitive fireworks displays

– I can safely, and guilt-free – root for all things Team America.

In the studio

Speaking of the athletes, I am one of maybe seven people in the country that actually enjoys the in-studio interviews. If the interviewer handles it well, I love to hear about people who burn more calories before 4:00AM every day than I do in a calendar year.

"So, after I finish running the stadium stairs at the Los Angeles Coliseum, I'll jog out to Joshua Tree National Park to run one of the trails. I make a game out of it! I'll throw a dart at the trail map and run the one closest to the dart. Twice."

Me? I will check to see if the closest KFC is still running their extra-oily/somewhat crispy 8-piece special. I do not feel bad if the interviewed athletes do not win, even after getting to know them. All of them have corporate law and/or finance jobs lined up for after the closing ceremonies. I guess you get a law degree if you just get a medal – it does not have to be gold.

Of course, some of these interviews can go south in a hurry. I have no idea what leads to this – bad day? Lost a bet on that fencing duel? – but sometimes, the interviewer will go nuts and spend 10+ minutes on every piece of misfortune to ever befall the person sitting in front of them. Even taking time to follow up with morbidly dark queries like: "No, really. What did it feel like to know that you would never see her grow up? Never see her smile again? Fall in love? Get Married? Have kids? Own a large boat? What was that *really* like?"

At that point, the athlete, fighting back a torrent of tears, will just stare blankly at the interviewer as if to say: "I thought we were just going to talk about how hard it is to get splashed and tread water..."

The Olympic mix

So here we are again, a colorful potpourri.

The good:

"And Paddy McKillarney win's Ireland's first ever gold medal in taekwondo! They said it couldn't be done, but he overcame a ton of adversity and the ban on groin kicks to finally do it!"

The bad:

"The Qatari rider's horse is actually trying to eat him..."

"Yeah, he'll lose some points from the judges for that."

"You know, that really doesn't happen at the upper levels of equestrian very often anymore."

"At least this isn't a tiger equestrian!"

"Not helpful, Jim."

The ugly:

"What did you do with your new fiancée's engagement ring after they fished her arm out of the alligator's stomach? Talk about lucky! What are the odds that they'd actually find the gator?"

(This Olympic themed essay is brought to you by Fannie's Ceiling Fans: Keeping writers who write in the summertime cool without the unnecessary use of Captain Cool's Air Conditioning since early this morning!)

Body Art - A Meaningful Tattoo

"If you begin to understand what you are without trying to change it, then what you are undergoes a transformation." - Jiddu Krishnamurti

Humans have an obsession with subcutaneous ink: Tattoos. What does it say about our species that we learned how to permanently etch memorials to bad decisions into our skin eons before we figured out the internal combustion engine, how to clone sheep, or how to beat Super Mario Brothers 3?

"Ah, in this cave painting we have an ancient Cro-Magnon police report. It appears that she struck the fatal blow mere seconds after discovering that the male had a tattoo of another woman on his left ass-cheek."

Still, despite the tattoo's checkered past, a history laden with moments of impulsive idiocy, I have always wanted a tattoo. It is a similar feeling to wanting a boat.

"Why do you want a boat?"

"You ever drive past a marina? Look how many boats there are! Practically everyone has a boat. I figure I should get in on that."

"What are you going to do with a boat? You don't even fish."

"Well, once or twice a year I'll take it out, get dehydrated and sunburnt while floating. The rest of the year I'll just pay a ton of money to have someone maintain/store it for me."

243

"Can't you just do all that in a pool? Why do you need a boat?"

"To throw your body overboard after I wallop your nosy little ass with the anchor."

But I digress.

I catch tattoo fever

By the age of 18, I was convinced that having a tattoo was another milestone on the road to unbridled success, along with a sweet car, a sweet stereo, and lots of Compact Discs. I had the car ('97 Camaro), the stereo/speakers (Onkyo, Polk, etc.), and hundreds of music storage items that would soon be obsolete. Only one thing remained...

However, in a rare - for that time period in my life - flash of self-awareness, I realized that I was not mature enough to commit to a lifetime of ill-conceived body art. I could handle the commitment of a 5-year car loan, but a lifetime was a bridge too far.

That is not to say I did not try to conjure up a nifty design. Deep reflection on the matter revealed several core issues with my first idea: a panoramic shot of the red Teletubby doing a flip off a large dune in the deserts of southern Tunisia. To start, I am not a large person. In order to get the shoulder-to-shoulder span of the desert, plus the size of the dune, the Teletubby and his/her dune buggy would have to be pretty small. So small, in fact, that someone would have to be five feet or less away from me to see that it was the red tubby. If someone cannot tell which PBS character I had permanently etched into my acne-covered back from at least 10 yards, what are we even doing here?

The second candidate to steam its way down the Bad Idea Railroad met its demise for more practical reasons. I had become enamored with dragons, thanks to the logo of the ramen brand I favored, since it was still decades before the dragons of How to Train Your Dragon would nestle their way into our hearts. Immediately, getting a sweet dragon permanently engraved on my torso became the tattoo priority. Having learned my lesson from before, I started with a plan that was a little more reserved: a large, polychromatic dragon emerging from my front waistband, lavishly looking to snarf down my left nipple. Once again, a dearth of real estate became an issue. Plus, the level of detail I demanded (forked tongues are necessary when getting a dragon tat) would quickly exceed my budget - $5 - for the project.

The tattoo wilderness

It would take 20+ more years of wandering this earth before I came up with something that was meaningful, sensible, and wouldn't scare anyone (unless they had an irrational fear of Greek architecture). In the interim, the closest I came was a piece featuring Donald Duck getting arrested for indecent exposure. (Put down the booze and put on some pants, Duck.) Per usual, Google helpfully gave me a list of local shops. I immediately slotted the shop with several misspelled words in its name at the bottom of the list. Even though I was not getting any words done, well...you know...optics.

All of the portfolios of the various artists that I considered featured some mix of the macabre, impossibly proportioned women in various states of undress, or some random design with spider webs ("A rose with a spider web? Bravo! A spider web with a spider web? C'est magnifique!"). This was going to have to be a B.Y.O.I. (Bring Your Own Image) endeavor. Once again, Google to the rescue. In .03 seconds, the search engine proudly returned more than 130 million hits.

The website of the place I settled on advertised that they accepted walk-ins. However, when I arrived to walk in, I was told that walk-ins are by appointment only. Flummoxed, I could almost feel a swell of respect for such a silly process. A respect for the purveyors who had come up with this and made an appointment to walk in a few hours later. Being a very hot day, my car lodged its displeasure over the additional workload by turning on the "check engine" light.

When I returned, a different person was manning the desk. He asked what I needed, and I proudly announced that I was here for a 3PM appointment to walk in. He was totally unmoved by the absurdity of what I had just said and simply whipped out a personal information form. Again, more respect.

The tattoo shop

The shop is in a fine American-style strip mall, wedged in between a girls' dance studio and a day spa. Other inhabitants include three ethnic markets: Asian, Central American, and just generic "international". With a minimal amount of walking, one can get authentic Szechuan spices, homemade tortillas, and whatever the hell Canada is known for.

The place was manned by three people – two artists and a third gentleman whose primary responsibility appeared to be acquiring various flavors of chips and energy drinks. I was a little worried about jumpy hands when I saw all the empty cans that had recently held 2.3 liters of sugar-infused caffeine. That concern was quickly assuaged when I saw how much they all smoked.

These guys made chimneys blush and talk in hushed tones. "Seriously, I think that chubby one has more creosote in his lungs than I do after three winters without a good sweep..."

When I left, I saw a team of beleaguered lung specialists taking cover from the heat of the day under a large shade tree as they passed a bottle of antidepressants amongst themselves – thinly disguised by a brown paper bag. With an air of despair, they spoke openly about ritual suicide.

My artist certainly looked the part. The only parts of his skin that were not covered in ink were his face and a thin band of visible skin between the bottom of his t-shirts and the top of his shorts. After a very quick consultation ("This is what I want." "So, like, this?" "Yep." "Cool.") we scheduled an appointment to get it done...for 5 minutes later.

Amusingly, by the time my appointment rolled around – 300 seconds (about 5 minutes) – he was "running behind" on account of a smoke break and the time needed to set up his station. No worries – it was less time than the average doctor's appointment, and the chairs were surprisingly comfortable. He is a really nice guy, and we chatted throughout the process.

The process itself was not bad at all. I am a self-avowed pain wuss, and I only winced once or twice. Even then, that was due more to an unexpected jab. I have no idea why my right calf needs to get involved when the tattoo is on my left forearm, but this guy seemed to know his profession. I'd be pretty pissed off if he came into my office – by appointment, of course – and told me how to do my job.

In fact, the most painful part was the movie they had running in the background. It was some action/thriller/spy movie starring two people I didn't know, Eric from That 70's Show, and dialogue that would make mid-80's Arnold Schwarzenegger cringe. I briefly flirted with the idea of saying something derogatory about the "writing", but quickly moved on from that notion for fear that the Sultan of the Snack Run would throw a bag of polyunsaturated fat at me, potentially ruining the vintage Bayern Munich jersey I was wearing.

All said, it did not take long. In roughly 90 minutes, this was on my arm:

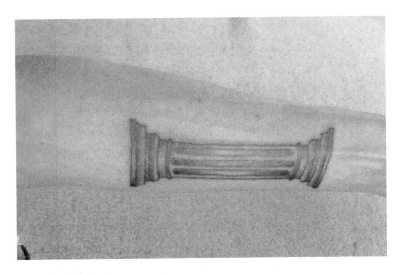

My tattoo 1

About halfway through I thought to get a "before" picture, but by then it was too late. No matter. If you just imagine the image above without a tattoo, you pretty much get the gist of it. You are only missing a few moles that are rapidly devolving into skin cancer after decades of lackadaisical UV protection. Maybe being covered in ink will buy me some time for those guys, especially the one that glows and trips off Geiger counters?

Tattoo aftermath

We returned to the stylish waiting area to settle up, and I could see a flash of light ignite behind his eyes when I mentioned that I'd pay with cash. Almost like a realization that said: "Cash - the form of payment I can get out of reporting to the Federalis...". As I turned to leave, I asked if I needed to schedule an exit appointment. He looked at me as if I was a special kind of moron. Either these guys are hardcore married to the bit, or they really don't know the difference between a "walk-in" and an "appointment".

When I got home, my wife was visibly relieved that I had stuck to the planned "simple Doric column" and had not gone rogue and switched it up to "garish graphic retelling of Gandalf vs. The Balrog". My youngest was flummoxed by the permanency of the situation. "It's like a sticker?" "Uhm...no." Oldest just asked to play video games. However, a few hours later, he announced – and this is not a joke – that he wanted to get a huge snake wrapped around his arm, with a picture of Saturn, and a B for Baltimore.

"When you're 18, bud...and even then, maybe take some time to think about it. Those tattoo removal lasers are no joke. Remember the Death Star (both of them)?"

Ah, youth...

But I understand. I took every opportunity to show off the new ink.

My tattoo 2

The Coda to this Symphony

"My soul is a hidden orchestra; I know not what instruments, what fiddlestrings and harps, drums and tamboura I sound and clash inside myself. All I hear is the symphony."

- Fernando Pessoa

This is the coda to my first scattershot symphony of musings and stories, all written during my transition from moribund office zombie to vibrant teacher/father/husband. In time, I will mash all of these together and bind them into what is known in the publishing industry as a "book". It would be one of the first times I have ever seen a project from start to finish, and I hope it will not be the last. This particular symphony ends in New York City, where my family and I just spent three days on a mini vacation.

It is a good locale in which to stop, as the whole trip distills down some of the transitional themes to a brisk 72 hours/1,400 words or so. I am not a fan of big cities – they are (obviously) large, with lots of people going in many directions, burning tons of energy in a wholly uncoordinated manner. But for Central Park, there are very few trees, lots of lights, and ample opportunity to spend thousands of dollars on a small bag designed to hold a wallet and/or small mammal.

In short, it is precisely the set up that was, for so many years, apt to raise my blood pressure, agitate the snot out of me, and generally turn me into a seven-year-old kid who just wants to go home and play video games.

One of the main potential points for agitation was Times Square at night. On the approach to the square itself, neon signs that measured in square miles were telling me how awesome the new Disney movie *Jungle Cruise* was. The taxis, bustling about and somehow avoiding pedestrian casualties, were proclaiming the same on the advertising space super glued to the roofs of their cabs. If you knew nothing about the human species but what you had learned walking from Madison Square Garden to Times Square, you'd think that all humans walked through traffic like drunken ants and that *Jungle Cruise* was the single greatest artistic/cultural experience of our sad civilization. Times "Square" itself is not really a square at all – rather, it is a series of irregular quadrilaterals. While this is an irritant, it is surmountable.

One of the main aspects of the "square" that did cause agitation reared its head was the open area. This area had robust looking cement barricades to keep taxis out and add a – welcome – sense of physical safety. So safe, in fact that people can congregate. As of this writing, I do not know what was going on in the "square", but it had the tell-tale sign of a phalanx of people with their cell phones out, taking video of whatever was going on. Aside from the first people to arrive on scene, no one could possibly

figure it out. A group of shirtless men who must
have spent lots of time in the gym were running
in ovals and yelling things into a microphone
that had the same sound quality of those toy
megaphones you can get a kid that play Paw
Patrol sounds while the kid babbles orders to
Rubble.

Still, the cellphone-razzi were wrapped
up in whatever was going on – street
performance, poetry reading protest, etc. In order
to cover all of my bases, I moonwalked for a few
meters, recited a line – with much gusto – from
an Emily Dickenson poem, and demanded an
immediate review of the United States Postal
Service's Publication 52, specifically Section
One, which governs the legal and illegal usage of
the USPS to mail live animals. Naturally, given
the hyper-political mindset that has strangled the
United States, someone tried to get into an
argument with me on how to determine the true
– for postal purposes – date of birth for a reptile.

Another point-of-interest we hit was the
Brooklyn Bridge. Many websites – most of
whom had advertisements for the new Disney
classic *Jungle Cruise* – told us that the bridge
was free to walk, offered superb views of
Manhattan, and was a modern engineering
marvel. The first part checked out. It was free
(or, at least, no one was there to take my money).

The second part was superlative. Halfway across the bridge, you could turn and look back to see the skyline of Manhattan, Governor's Island, and even the Statue of Liberty.

I do take issue with the claim of engineering marvel. That bridge is far from flat. The first part, from Manhattan to the centerline, is all uphill. And not just a little either – that is a pretty steep grade. The Millard Tydings Bridge over the Susquehanna River in northeast Maryland is also a body of water. Though admittedly not as aesthetically appealing, at least it is as flat as a pancake. That, dear friends, is an engineering marvel.

Of course, we went to Central Park. There is not very much irksome about that place except that it is exactly like ten or so parks right around my house. The only difference between Central Park and the park around Lake Elkhorn near my house is a really sweet zip code. Everything else is about the same. The only real difference is actually more amusing than irritating. Whereas we have foot-driven paddle boats, where 2-out-of-2 occupants can propel the vessel, Central Park has row boats. In New York we saw many a young lad, who was completely unfamiliar with rowing an oar-driven boat, try to impress his date by getting that thing out and back in a reasonable amount of time in a reasonably straight line.

We also tackled two of the main museums – the Metropolitan Museum of Art and the Natural History Museum. They had time-based entry tickets but still required a hefty period of waiting time, with actual entry well past the appointed time. Both had spectacular exhibits that had me daydreaming about them coming to life and taking care of some of the crowds for me. And I do not just mean the paintings of armed people at the Met and dinosaurs with spikes, large teeth, and disproportionately small heads and/or arms. I included the gentle looking gnus, the non-venomous (but still scary looking) invertebrates of the history museum. At the Met, the naked ladies who had clearly been day drinking when their image was carved into marble were in play.

There was, however, a moment of Zen. I am the kind of driver that is more in the "Eh, we are almost to the exit/turn. Just stay in this lane – no need to go around" school of thought. Taxi drivers are not. So, while a taxi driver (who looked nothing like his posted license) was bobbing and weaving from our hotel to Columbus Circle we came upon this scene while stuck in traffic:

A foreman was planning out the day for a new crew he was working with. He asked one of the more seasoned crew members "When do you usually eat lunch on this shift?" The crew member replied: "Honestly..." and trailed off.

Immediately, the foreman jumped in with: "Honestly? No I want you to lie to me moron. That'll go well."

In the office world this is how that conversation would play out:

"When do you want to eat lunch?"

"Honestly...it doesn't really matter. Anytime between 11:00AM and 3:00PM."

"Ok. How about 12:30?"

"Oh! I have a meeting with the director of life animal mailing enforcement then. 11:30?"

"Nah - I might need you to cover down on the staff meeting with Chuck's people."

<five minutes of playing with smartphones>

"Got it – how about I just steal a bite after the mail people?"

"Perfect."

It calmed my nerves to see a wonderfully efficient and honest conversation.

There is much more from the trip to New York City – as mentioned, it is a big city – but I will not belabor the point. Most of the stuff was the foibles of Marylanders visiting an unfamiliar big city. We've all been there, if you're a Marylander, of course... Instead, I will close with this:

In years gone by these things, the un Zen-like annoyances, and an army of smaller ones not worth mentioning would cause my spine to tingle, my breathing to speed up, and initiate a sharp desire to grab one or several stiff drinks. But, thanks to this road of transition that my wife started me down years ago, when she started to plan for me to leave the office and chase dreams – a journey of learning to be content where I was when I was there – I felt none of those sensations of duress. This is a good thing. A very good thing. I may have forgotten to mention this earlier, but...

I am a recovering alcoholic.

Acknowledgements

I will be 41 when this gets published. It has always been a dream of mine to write a book. So, some acknowledgements are in order. Leah Chrest was the content editor and made things flow. Linda Boschert is the copy editor who minds all my Ps and Qs for me. If this book is not good, it is because of my content and not because there are all kinds of typos. Brooks and Brandon aggressively volunteered to play lots of video games so I could think. Finally, I acknowledge all of the Hal's out there who popped up to make me appreciate how meaningful the absurd can be.

About the author

Nicholas B. Chrest was born September 4, 1980. On or about September 5th, 1980, he adopted "Brett" as his nom de guerre and started telling stories. His first positive reviews came from the nursery staff for his recounting of the trip down the birth canal.

He was an office zombie, and became an educator to teach the joy of writing.

He reads philosophy for fun and is mostly known for being rather boring.

Made in the USA
Monee, IL
04 September 2021